MILNER CRAFT SERIES

EXQUISITE EMBROIDERY

MILNER CRAFT SERIES

EXQUISITE EMBROIDERY

JENNIFER NEWMAN

SALLY MILNER PUBLISHING

First published in 1993 by
Sally Milner Publishing Pty Ltd
558 Darling Street
Rozelle NSW 2039 Australia

© Jennifer Newman, 1993

Design by Wing Ping Tong
Photography by Andrew Elton
Typeset in Australia by Asset Typesetting Pty Ltd
Printed in Australia by Impact Printing, Melbourne

National Library of Australia
Cataloguing-in-Publication data:

Newman, Jennifer, 1960–
    Exquisite embroidery.

    ISBN 1 86351 079 6.

    1. Embroidery. 2. Embroidery — Patterns. I. Title.
    (Series: Milner craft series).

746.44

ONTENTS

ACKNOWLEDGEMENTS

In the time that I have been writing this book, I have been assisted by many people who have generously shared their ideas and suggestions. Among them have been students in my workshops, fellow teachers and designers, and people who have written to me following magazine articles in *Sew Beautiful*. There are so many that it is impossible to name them all, so to all those wonderful helpers, I thank you.

There have been a number of people, without whom, I would never have been motivated to write this book, much less finish it. They are:

Martha Pullen, who took a completely unknown Australian designer and risked publishing my work through her fabulous magazine *Sew Beautiful*. Her commitment to continuing to publish my designs was my inspiration to write.

During my research for this book I found what turned out to be an excellent article on needles. It was written in French, and rather beyond my linguistic capabilities. Beth Sergeant painstakingly translated this for me. Her time and effort were greatly appreciated.

Joyce Oakley, of Capitol Imports Inc. supplied the majority of fabric and trims for this publication. Her generosity and enthusiasm, as well as her beautiful products, helped me enormously.

Pam Courtney, an Australian who dyes her own floss, hand-dyed thread for use on the face washer and hand towel. She altered her product to suit my needs, which has taken considerable time and experimentation on her part.

Ann Evans, Katrina and Cathy Cahill generously loaned me interesting props for photography. Cathy organised the acquisition of these and their return. She has been supportive and wonderfully helpful and I thank her.

The delicious picnic food that is photographed with the hats was provided by Bonds Corner Fine Foods, 395 Sailors Bay Road, Northbridge. They can be contacted on (02) 958 3432.

The magnificent flowers were generously supplied by Lisa Milasas. Lisa can be contacted on (02) 524 8918.

Andrew Elton did a great job photographing the embroidery. His attention to detail and skill with lighting was much appreciated.

Andrew and Julie Elton allowed their beautiful three-month-old daughter, Lauren, to model the baby day gown. She looked gorgeous and behaved impeccably.

Julie Elton, in between caring for a young baby and coping with a photo shoot at her house, did my make-up for the portrait shots. I am indebted to her for making me look decent.

Louise Owens did the styling for the photography. She was so organised and managed to chase down some much needed props. Her wonderful quiet nature as well as her artistic ability ensured the success of the photo shoot.

Sally Milner, the publisher of this book, has been very supportive over the past 15 months. She and Marg Bowman have listened with patience to my ideas and have ultimately moulded my work into a book. Their dedication and enthusiasm has sustained me many times when I was ready to give up.

Barb Griffin, a designer and author of two books whom I met on a brief trip to the USA, seems to have always been there, at the other end of the telephone line. She advised, encouraged and listened. I am indebted to her for the numerous jobs she has done but most of all for her friendship and positive attitude. Barb could always make me see the funny side of my most dire mistakes (and I have made lots of them).

Louisa Cooper, my dear friend and talented smocker, has shopped for me, listened to my latest ideas, helped me with construction that I was unsure about; all with patience and enthusiasm. It has been great to have such a close friend with whom to share my thoughts.

Lyn Weeks, who is an Australian smocking designer and teacher, has done much to help me with this book. She has read instructions and offered suggestions and constructive criticism, as well as searching out much needed supplies. I cherish her support and friendship.

Dianne Akers, my sister, has been there to support and advise me since I started writing. She has spent so much time helping me with designs, instructions and layout she should almost be co-author.

My mother, Hazel Newman, who taught me to sew in the first place. She is largely responsible for the love I have of this craft. Mum also thought of the name for this book just when I was at the desperate and dejected stage.

Vicki Binks, my office manager and friend, has handled my practice with professionalism and patience. I know it is not easy to deal with a boss who wants to have a full-time job and write a book simultaneously. Her efficiency has allowed me the mental 'space' to concentrate on writing.

John Mongan, my husband, who has coped for as long as I can remember with my sewing mess. He rarely complains about walking on pins, typing yet another article or having to cook dinner. With a great deal of patience and love he taught me to use a word processor. He has supported me from one crazy idea to the next and managed to keep us both sane and laughing. Without him this book would never have been finished.

INTRODUCTION

Writing a book has been one of the most demanding, frustrating and wonderful experiences I have ever had. I never expected it to be as it was. Along the way my life has been touched by many people I would never normally have met. Many of them have asked me what *Exquisite Embroidery* is about.

This deserves an answer and is an excellent way to introduce my book.

Exquisite Embroidery is about many things. It's a beginners guide to embroidery, a text on some of the technical aspects of sewing, and a compilation of some new designs. But, most of all, it is a celebration of the joy that embroidery has brought me.

Many people feel daunted by the prospect of embroidering a gift. They question their ability (a feeling that I am well aware of, having spent most of my life doing it!) and whether the recipient of their work will like and appreciate it.

In a world where so many experiences are overrated and time is our most valuable commodity, I have found that a handmade gift says it all. An embroidered gift should never be judged on technical excellence but on the fact that someone thought enough to spend a lot of their time to produce something unique. If you are new to embroidery, then do not feel frustrated that some of your stitches are not perfect. Instead, think of the time and love you have put into them. Nothing can ever replace or surpass that.

Many students of embroidery feel that teachers were born knowing what to do and did not have to go through the frustrating process of learning. I can assure you that I was taught what I know, and indeed am still learning (mostly from my students). I still agonise over the best way to do something and I still have designs that don't work.

Writing this book has led me to believe that in embroidery, there are no rights or wrongs, just differences and preferences. Have confidence in your own judgement.

Exquisite Embroidery covers lots of aspects of handsewing, but most of all it's about teaching people to have a go and to love what they do. If this book gives you a new idea or teaches you something you thought that you could never learn, then I have achieved my aim.

ENLARGING PATTERNS

A number of the patterns in this book need to be enlarged. There are many methods for doing this, but the easiest is to use one of today's modern photocopiers. Two methods for using photocopies to get exact enlargements are given below.

METHOD ONE

Many 'state of the art' photocopiers permit the user to set the exact enlargement they require. If you have access to one of these, then use this method.

On all patterns and embroidery designs you are told what size they are relative to the original if they have been reduced. For example, the face washer design is 80% of its original size. Using the table below, you look up 80% and see that the photocopier needs to be set at a 125% enlargement to produce a design of the right size.

Size of pattern relative to original	Photocopier must be set to enlarge by this percentage
60%	166%
65%	154%
70%	143%
75%	133%
80%	125%
85%	117%
90%	111%
95%	105%

Small differences in percentages, for example 164% to 166%, will have little bearing on the pattern size.

METHOD TWO

If you have access to a photocopier that enlarges but are unable to set exact enlargements, it is still possible to get a pattern of the right size with a simple measurement and calculation. This method will also work where you want to enlarge a design to a certain size.

Choose a straight line position on the pattern or design and measure it (preferably in millimetres). If possible, it is best to draw this line on the pattern. The distance you measure could be the width of the pattern or even the distance between two bows.

In this book you are told the size of the pattern given relative to the original. Using the table below look up the multiplication factor for your particular enlargement.

Size of pattern relative to original	Multiplication factor
60%	1.66
65%	1.54
70%	1.43
75%	1.33
80%	1.25
85%	1.17
90%	1.11
95%	1.05

Your calculation will be this:
New Measurement (in mm) = Old measurement (in mm) multiplied by multiplication factor from table. Let's look at an example.

On page 77, the width of the hat band design is 30 mm. We are told this design is 75% of the size of the original. We look up the multiplication factor for 75% and find it is 1.33.

Our calculation looks like this:
New measurement
     = 30 x 1.33
     = 39.9 mm — or very close to 40 mm

Once this calculation is made, keep enlarging the pattern on the photocopier until the straight line position you have chosen measures the same (approximately) on the enlarged copy as your calculation.

GETTING TO THE POINT

Needles are an essential tool of the embroiderer's trade. What needle to use and its size are mainly a matter of personal choice, but there are some broad guidelines to bear in mind.

Needles should make a hole in the fabric large enough for the eye and the thread to pass through comfortably. Indications that this is not happening are:

1. The thread quickly wears thin.
2. Resistance when pulling the thread through the fabric.

If either or both these occur, try changing to a larger needle of the same type. If the only problem is the thread wearing thin quickly, try a needle with a larger eye or keep the same needle and use a shorter length of thread.

A needle that is too large will leave a hole in the fabric that the thread does not fill. Sometimes this effect is desirable for decorative purposes such as pin stitch, which is usually worked with a size 6 crewel or size 24 tapestry needle. However, if it is not desirable, change to a smaller needle.

As a general rule, it is better to use a needle that is slightly too large than one that is too small. Master new stitches with large needles and thick threads and then reduce both as your technique improves.

Needles must be straight and have undamaged points. Throw out bent and corroded ones; they make uneven stitches and damage the fabric. Keep a good supply of your favourites and store them in a clean, dry place. Needles are best left in their packets until ready to be used. A strawberry emery, available at the haberdashery section of most fabric shops, is handy for keeping needles sharp.

To understand which needle to use, let's study their 'anatomy'.

Needles have five major features that help determine the stitches they produce:

Eye of the needle
Point of the needle
Length of the needle
Width of the shaft
Variation in diameter or curvature of the shaft

To help identify the appropriate needle for a particular job, there is a set of names denoting certain features.

The most common of these names are:

Crewel or embroidery
Betweens or Quilters
Tapestry
Sharps
Chenille
Beading
Darning
Straw or Milliners
Easy threading or calyx
Bodkins
Ballpoint

Some of the more uncommon groups of needles are:

Darners
Long darners
Leather or Glovers
Sailmakers or Bookbinders
Sack or Upholstery
Mattress or Lampshade
Doll

Manufacturers also give sizes to their needles. This size refers to the diameter of the shaft and the length of the needle. The larger the number, the shorter and finer the needle. For example, any type or size 10 would be finer and shorter than a size 3 of the same type.

Needle sizing does not seem to be consistent throughout the industry and there is also variation within ranges from the same manufacturer. Experimentation, rather than blind belief in what is written on the packet, is the best guide.

EYE OF THE NEEDLE

Here are the four most common eyes:

1. Round Eye

2. Long Eye

3. Elongated or Tapestry

4. Calyx

POINTS OF NEEDLES

Here are the four most common points:

1. Normal, Sharp Point

2. Blunt

3. Ballpoint

4. Triangular

Table 1 lists all the major needle types, their characteristics and primary uses. It is intended as a reference to guide you through the multitude of needles available.

Remember; trust in your own judgement. If you find a brand and type of needle you like working with for particular sewing tasks, stick with it.

In the chapters on embroidery stitches, I have listed needles that I like using, but these are only suggestions because personal preference is the most important factor.

Table of Needle Characteristics and Uses

Common name of needle	Eye	Point	Characteristics of shaft	Sizes available	Special features	Common uses
Sharps	round eye	normal sharp	medium	3-12	Short, round eye gives added strength to needle	General-purpose handsewing for most fabrics
Crewel or embroidery	long eye	normal sharp	medium	3-10	Long eye allows more than one strand of floss to be threaded in needle	Nearly all hand-embroidery stitches can be worked with this needle. Useful for smocking
Betweens or Quilters	round eye	normal sharp	short	3-10	The short length facilitates fine stitches into heavy fabric	Traditionally used by quilters and tailors for quick, even stitching. Needle used by the embroiderers of Madeira (size 9)
Tapestry	elongated or tapestry	blunt	medium	18-24	Heavy needles with blunt ends do not split fabric threads	Wool embroidery on fabric or canvas. Most forms of canvas work
Chenille or Couching	elongated or tapestry	normal sharp	medium	18-24	Very heavy-duty needle	Chenille work, stitching thick yarns onto coarse fabric
Straw or Milliners	small round	normal sharp	long	3-10	Long shaft that does not vary in diameter from eye of the needle until it tapers at the point. There is no bulge at the eye — it is totally contained within the shaft	Embroidery stitches that involve the wrapping of thread around the shaft of the needle, e.g. bullion stitch and french knots. The consistent diameter produces even stitches and the long shaft allows room for many wraps
Ballpoint	round	ballpoint	medium	3-9	Ballpoint slides between fibres of knit to prevent laddering or other damage	Sewing knitted fabrics such as interlock, jersey, etc
Beading	long	normal sharp	very long and thin	10-15	Because of its length, beads can easily be threaded on this needle. Can bend easily	Beading and sequin work

Common name of needle	Eye	Point	Characteristics of shaft	Sizes available	Special features	Common uses
Easy threading or Calyx eye	calyx	normal sharp	medium	4–8	Thread is pulled into a slot rather than threaded through the eye	General-purpose sewing as for sharps. Especially useful for those who have difficulty threading needles
Bodkins	often 2 eyes. Round and long	blunt	thick straight	2 sizes	Size is dependent on nature of yarn and material being worked	To thread elastic, tape or cord
Darner	long	normal sharp	long	1–8 or 14–18 wool darners	Long shaft allows you to span holes	Darning all weights of fabric
Long darners or double longs	long	normal sharp	very long	1–8	Very long shaft makes darning large holes possible	Darning larger holes that could not be done with a normal darner
Leather or Glovers	round	triangular	medium	3–8	Triangular point pierces leather, vinyl and plastic without tearing	Sewing plastics, leather and vinyl
Sailmakers or Book-binders	long	triangular that goes half way up shaft	medium	14–17	Extension of triangular point makes handling of heavy fabric easier	Sewing heavy fabrics such as canvas, heavy vinyl and leather
Sack or upholstery	long	wedge shape	curved, and wedge extends to end of curve	2 sizes	Curved shaft allows more inaccessible areas to be stitched	Stitching upholstery and some weaving
Mattress or Lampshade	long	normal sharp	curved, semi circular	3–8 cm (1″–3″) length	Curved shaft allows inaccessible areas to be stitched	Upholstering including seats, lampshades and rugs
Doll	long	normal sharp	very long	8–18 cm (3″–7″) length	Long shaft allows stitching through great thicknesses	Doll making

HREADS

All natural fibres must be spun to produce threads.

The fibres can be spun in one of two ways:

1. Clockwise
2. Anti- or counter-clockwise.

The direction of spinning produces a characteristic twist to the thread.

If the spinning wheel is turned clockwise, a 'Z' twist is produced.

Diagram 1

If the spinning wheel is turned anti-clockwise, an 'S' twist is produced.

Diagram 2

The next step in the manufacturing process involves the individual spun threads being 'plied' to form a yarn or floss with the requisite strength.

If the fibres are initially spun with a 'Z' twist, they must be plied with an 'S' twist in order to prevent over-twisting of the finished thread.

In the case of stranded floss thread, cotton fibres are spun with a 'Z' twist to form some very fine threads. Two of these very fine threads are plied with an 'S' twist to produce one strand of floss. The manufacturer then loosely twists six of these single strands together to give the six-strand embroidery floss with which we are all familiar.

When one strand of floss is separated from the five other strands, it behaves as an 'S' twist thread because that was the last spinning process applied to the thread before use.

Threads that behave as 'S' twists because of plying include DMC floss and all other brands of embroidery cotton, perle cotton, tapestry wool, Medici and crewel wool as well as Madeira silk floss.

Threads which behave as 'Z' twists include many of the Brazilian rayon threads and some silk threads such as Kanagawa 1000.

As embroiders, we cannot change the way thread is made but we need to take into consideration its twist when we are stitching. This twist of thread influences the result when stitches are formed.

Being able to identify the twist of the thread allows you to predict the look of a finished stitch. For example, suppose you are using three strands of DMC floss to do outline stitch (remember that DMC floss behaves as an 'S' twist thread). If you stitch from left to right and the thread is held above the needle, the thread will wrap in the same direction as the twist of the thread. This will produce an outline stitch with a smooth appearance.

Diagram 3

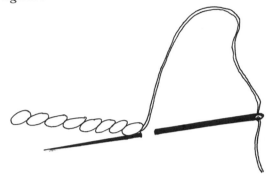

A smooth bullion is formed with an 'S' twist thread by wrapping the thread anti-clockwise around the needle. A corded effect is obtained by winding the thread clockwise.

It is fun to experiment with different threads. Try wrapping them both ways and decide what effect you like. Remember, there are no hard and fast rules about embroidery; different techniques produce different effects.

The reverse would be true for a thread behaving as a 'Z' twist.

If you stitch, with an 'S' twist thread with the thread below the needle, the stitch formed will wrap in the opposite direction to the twist of the thread. Instead of a smooth appearance, this stitch will be more 'corded'.

Diagram 4

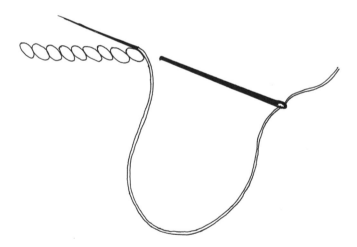

A smooth finish is obtained with a 'Z' twist thread by holding the thread under the needle while stitching.

These instructions are given for right-handers stitching from left to right. Of course, the reverse is true for left-handers who are stitching from right to left.

Whether a corded or smooth stitch is required is an artistic choice for the embroiderer. This 'directionality' of threads extends to and affects other wrapped stitches such as bullions.

ABRIC

Almost all fabric can be embroidered if correctly handled. If you are going to spend a lot of time stitching, it is well worth using good quality fabric.

Natural fibres have stood the test of time and are still the most beautiful to work on. As a beginner, it is sometimes easier to manage the thicker fabrics such as velveteen and woollen blanketing. As you refine your techniques, try working on fine fabric such as Swiss voile or batiste. The results are very rewarding. Of course, fabric must be matched to the type of embroidery you wish to do. Shadow work, for example, is never going to work on velvet. Silk is often seen as a difficult fabric but you will encounter few problems providing it is pre-washed and fraying is minimised by over-casting the edges.

Try, as far as possible, to match your chosen fabric with the threads being used. It makes a lot of sense to use silk threads on silk fabric, cotton on cotton fabric, and so on. I do use silk threads on cotton fabric to obtain a different effect, but this is the exception rather than the rule. Linen is a wonderful fabric to work on and cotton threads are ideal with it.

Good fabric should always be cut by pulling a thread to ensure the straight grain.

I like to wash fabric (silk included) before embroidering it, as this removes any dressing that the manufacturer may have used. It also gives me an idea of how the finished article is going to look after washing and wearing. If fabric does not wash well, it is better to select another to work on. Do not pre-wash woollen fabric, velvet or velveteen as these materials are best dry-cleaned. Fabric needs to be pressed and allowed to cool before the design is traced onto it.

OOPS

A hoop is one piece of equipment embroiderers either love or hate. I'm one of those who finds a hoop essential when working certain types of embroidery such as shadow work because it helps to keep the tension even.

The size of hoop required is dependent on the dimensions of the piece you intend to embroider. However, a good starting point is to choose a hoop from a range of 12.5 cm to 17.5 cm (5″ to 7″) in diameter. Wooden screw-type ones with the inner ring wrapped in bias tape are ideal. You can also use plastic ones which, generally, do away with the need for tape because fabric will not snag on their smooth surface. Plastic hoops also seem to allow the work to be pulled tighter, without damaging the fabric.

When very fine, delicate fabrics are to be worked, it is not a bad idea to cover even the plastic hoops to ensure the fabric remains in pristine condition. To do this, cut two circles of lightweight, non-woven interfacing about 5 cm (2″) larger in diameter than that of the hoop. That is, if you are using a 12.5 cm (5″) hoop, the diameter of the circles need to be about 17.5 cm (7″).

Place these two interfacing circles together and cut a circle from the middle approximately 8 cm (3″) in diameter to form two 'doughnut'-shaped pieces of interfacing.

Now place one 'doughnut' on the table. Put the fabric with the embroidery design traced on it on top and finish with the second 'doughnut'. Make sure that the embroidery design is visible through the hole in the interfacing. This triple layer is then 'loaded' into the hoop and none of the delicate fabric is in direct contact with the hoop.

Note: An excellent type of plastic hoop is made by Semco and the Susan Bates Company, and is my preference.

No matter what type of fabric is being used, it is important to remove the hoop from your work when you are not stitching. This allows the fabric to relax and prevents it being marked by the ring.

PREPARATION

PRODUCTS FOR TRACING A DESIGN ONTO FABRIC

There are many products available for tracing designs onto fabric. Which one you use depends on the colour of the fabric; transparency or opacity of the fabric; and the necessity to wash the fabric.

Whatever marker you use, it is best to test it on a scrap of fabric both for visibility and ease of removal before embarking on a major project.

The most common transfer materials are pencils or markers but dressmakers' carbon is also available.

1. BLUE WASHOUT MARKERS

These look like blue felt-tipped pens. The marks they make wash out in cold water. They are very handy for regular sewing tasks such as marking button holes. I sometimes use them on washable, opaque fabrics such as silk.

The main disadvantages of these pens are that the line they draw is fairly thick, and the colour of the pen distorts the colour of your work, so they are a nuisance if you are doing a sample to check colours. Also, ironing fabric will set the marks permanently.

2. PURPLE FADE-OUT MARKERS

These also look like felt-tipped markers but are purple. The marks made by these pens are air-erasable within 48-hours or they can be removed by rinsing in cold water. These marks are said to be removable even if ironed over but I would test a fabric sample before assuming this to be the case.

How quickly the purple marks disappear seems to depend on weather conditions. I have found that they last longer if sealed in a snap-lock bag when not being worked on.

I always like to rinse this pen out after I finish my project as I don't think it is good if unnecessary chemicals remain in the finished article.

These pens are of more use for regular sewing tasks than delicate embroidery because the line drawn is fairly thick, and your design can disappear before you have finished working it.

I sometimes use this pen if I am adding something to a design as I go along or if I am embroidering around a shape with no predetermined design.

3. CHALK-BASED MARKING PENCILS

These pencils generally come in pink, blue and white and sometimes yellow. The 'lead' in the pencil has a chalk base so it will just brush away. I find these handy on dark fabrics that you don't want to wash after the embroidery is complete. The colours are too pale for transferring designs onto light fabric. The line they draw tends to be fairly thick (even if sharpened to a fine point). Also, the chalk markers disappear if the work is handled a great deal.

4. SILVER AND WHITE MARKER PENCILS (ALSO CALLED QUILTER'S PENCILS)

These pencils have a very firm 'lead' and so sharpen to a fine point. Care needs to be exercised in using them because the very rigid point may damage delicate fabric. They produce a very fine line and can be removed with a fabric eraser. I have found that the marks from this sort of pencil do not wash out well. They are very useful for working on very dark fabrics.

5. HOT-IRON TRANSFER PENCILS

I never use this type of marker because it tends to 'bleed'; the line formed is thick and it is impossible to wash it out after the embroidery is completed.

6. LEAD PENCILS

Most people who use these recommend the harder lead pencils such as a 2H or a 3H and not HB or any of the B series. They give a fine line but are very difficult to wash out. If they are not removed completely, their colour dulls the finished work.

Removability is helped by heavily spray-starching the fabric before the design is traced on. If removal is still difficult, some of the heavy-duty stain removers such as Z'out or Allendale Stain Remover will usually complete the task.

There is a water-soluble graphite pencil now available which is better than a regular lead pencil. Art shops sometimes stock them; they are used by watercolour painters. I do not use graphite pencils very much in my work.

7. DIXON MARKERS

These look like regular lead pencils, but with coloured leads. They are available in blue, pink and sometimes white and green. Their leads can be sharpened to a fine point and they produce a fine design line. The marks they make are removed by washing in warm water. They generally wash out, even if ironed over, but I would check this on a sample before use on a project. Their main disadvantage is that, because they are chalk-based,

they tend to disappear if work is handled a great deal. Also, in order to keep a sharp point, it is necessary to keep sharpening the tip. I use these pencils extensively in my work.

8. DRESSMAKER'S CARBON OR EMBROIDERY TRACING PAPER

This tracing paper is sold under a variety of names and consists of an opaque sheet of paper that has carbon on one side. The carbon side is placed face down on the fabric with the desired design on top. The design is traced over using a ballpoint pen or pencil. This method produces a very definite line and is useful when dealing with dense, opaque fabrics where there are few other options for transferring a design. I have experienced some difficulties in washing out the marks made by the carbon, so it is essential to check on a sample before you begin. I use this product on the wrong side of velvet as there is no need to wash it out.

CENTRING A DESIGN ON THE FABRIC

I always work all the embroidery before cutting out the pattern pieces. I do this for the following reasons: Necklines and other delicate areas can be stretched while working the embroidery; some fabrics, such as silk dupion, have a tendency to fray when handled and washed, which is necessary when the embroidery is complete; when the embroidery design is worked, it often varies slightly from the initial traced design and this can be taken into account when the pattern piece is cut.

When tracing a design onto a fabric, always ensure there is sufficient room around the outside of the design to cut out the pattern piece to the required size. I like to leave between 3-8 cm (1"-3") of extra fabric beyond what is required. This gives plenty of room for small adjustments once the design is embroidered.

With most fabrics it is best to either zigzag or overlock the outside edge to prevent fraying.

Diagram 1

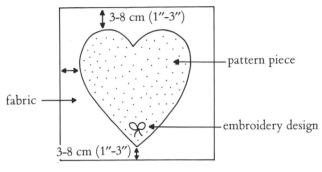

join

4. On some fabrics which have pile, such as velveteen, it is best to use dressmaker's carbon and to trace the design onto the wrong side of the fabric.

The method you use to transfer designs onto fabric is a personal choice. Try a few different methods and find out what works best for you and the materials of your choice.

TRACING A DESIGN ONTO FABRIC

1. It is a simple matter to trace the design of your choice onto fabric as long as the fabric is semi-transparent and the design is visible when placed underneath. A cork notice-board used as a tracing surface, with the fabric and design held down with pins, makes it possible to keep both the design and the fabric firm while the design is being transferred.

2. Sometimes it is necessary to have light coming from behind in order to be able to view the design through the fabric. If this is so in your case, trace the embroidery design onto a piece of tracing paper and tape it to a window. Tape the fabric in the correct position over the top of the design and trace with the appropriate marker.

3. If the fabric is very dense and opaque, such as wool blanketing, then prick the design with a large needle to form small, but regular, holes. Place the pricked paper in the desired position over the fabric and, using the marker of your choice, dot in these holes. When the paper is removed, a spotted outline will remain. These dots are then joined to give a solid outline.

GETTING STARTED

STITCHES

BACK STITCH

Back stitch is one of the basic utility stitches used in both embroidery and regular sewing.

1. To make a row of back stitches, bring needle up at A.

Diagram 1

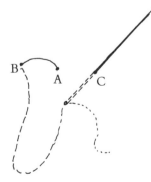

2. Insert needle at B and bring up again at C.

Diagram 2

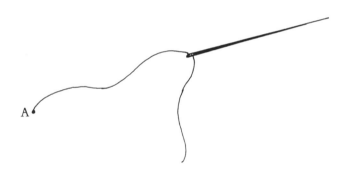

3. Reinsert needle in the same hole as before at A and bring up again at D (see diagram 3).

Diagram 3

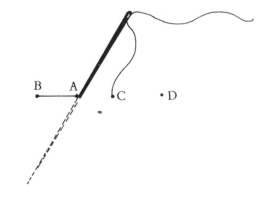

SPLIT BACK STITCH

A split back stitch is used to start off the stitch in preference to a knot. It can only be used in situations where the embroidery stitch used will cover the starting point.

1. Bring your thread from the wrong side of the work to the right side at A, ensuring that a 'tail' of thread 2–4 mm (⅟₁₆″–¼″) is left hanging on the wrong side.

Diagram 4

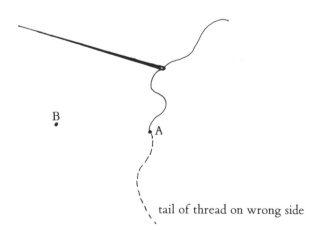

tail of thread on wrong side

2. Take a back stitch from A to B and bring the needle out at C. Ensure, as the needle comes out at C, that it pierces the tail of the thread that is hanging on the wrong side.

Diagram 5

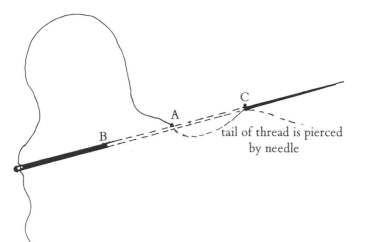

3. Take another stitch from C to A, pulling thread firmly. This is usually sufficient to secure the thread. If in doubt, repeat by going down at A and piercing the thread again while making another back stitch. When you are happy that the thread is secure, cut off the tail and commence stitching.

OUTLINE AND STEM STITCH

These are two very similar stitches. The difference is whether the thread is held above or below the needle. It doesn't matter what you call this stitch provided you achieve the effect that you want!

At school, we were always taught that in stem stitch, the thread is below the needle (as in nature, the stem is always UNDER the flower).

Later I was to realise that the look of the stitch was determined by two factors; where the thread was held and the twist of the thread.

As explained in the chapter on threads, embroidery threads have a characteristic twist. Threads such as DMC, Susan Bates, Semco floss, Madeira silk, and perle cotton all behave as 'S' twists. In order to achieve a smooth-looking line, the thread is held above the needle.

1. To stem stitch, secure the thread with a split back stitch (see page 24). Bring the thread out at A and reinsert the needle at B, with the thread held above the needle.

Diagram 6

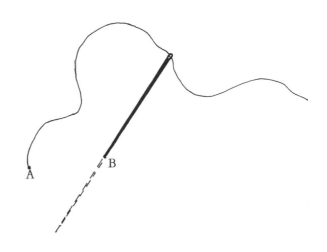

2. For the first stitch only, come up at C, halfway between A and B, making sure that the thread between A and B is above the needle.

Diagram 7

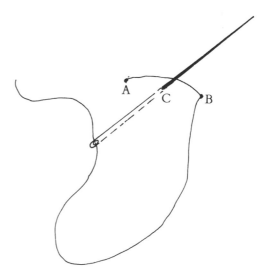

3. For all remaining stitches, the needle is brought out of the same hole as that of the previous stitch. That is, with the thread above the needle, stitch from C to D with the needle re-emerging at B (see diagram 8).

Diagram 8

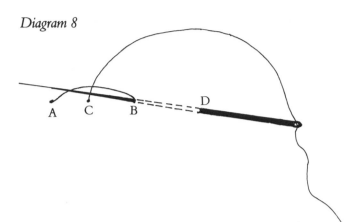

4. The stitch continues in this manner; that is, from B to E and re-emerging at D.

Diagram 9

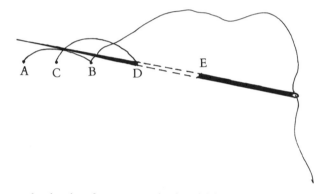

The back of your work should be a line of back stitches, regardless of whether the thread is held above or below the needle.

To achieve a corded stitch, the method is identical but the thread is held *under* the needle.

FEATHER STITCH

Feather stitch and its variations are beautiful additions to any embroiderer's repertoire.

It is a simple stitch, provided a few basic rules are followed.

In single feather stitch, one stitch is taken to the right and one to the left. In double feather stitch, two stitches are taken to the right and then two to the left — and so on for triple feather stitch.

No matter what type of feather stitch you are doing, unless you are experienced, rule parallel lines to guide you. For single feather stitch you will need four parallel lines.

The needle is brought out at A and a loop of thread is left between A and B. The needle is then placed in the fabric at B and re-emerges at C, catching the loop of thread there. Pull the loop so it lies flat.

Diagram 10

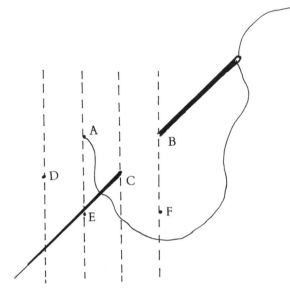

For the second stitch, the needle is inserted at D and emerges at E. Make sure that the thread is under the needle. The next stitch will see the needle inserted at F and emerging at G.

Diagram 11

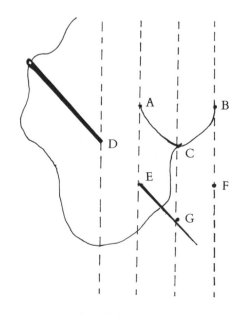

Continue in this fashion.

DOUBLE FEATHER STITCH

This is worked in identical fashion to single feather stitch except that two stitches are taken to the right, followed by two stitches to the left. Five parallel lines are needed as a guide.

Diagram 12

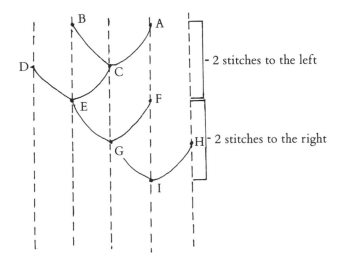

TRIPLE FEATHER STITCH

This stitch requires six parallel lines as a guide.

Diagram 13

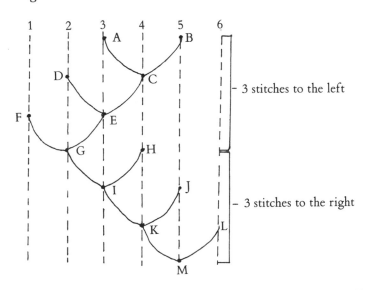

LAZY DAISY STITCH

This is a quick and easy stitch and is handy for leaves as well as flowers.

Start with the needle below the fabric. Bring it up at A and down as close as possible to the same point. A stitch is then taken between A and B and a loop of thread is caught.

Diagram 14

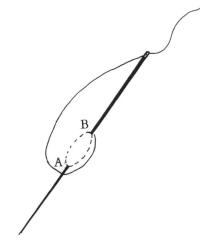

Pull the needle all the way through to tighten the loop. A small anchoring stitch is then taken between B and C: the needle comes out at B and re-enters the fabric at C, a short distance away.

Diagram 15

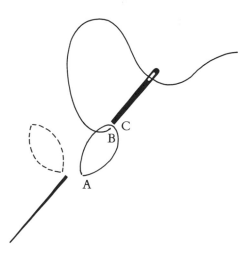

BUTTONHOLE STITCH

This is an extremely useful stitch, ideal for decoration or to finish off raw edges.

Begin by securing the thread on the wrong side of the work with a small split back stitch.

Bring the needle out on the line which is to have the perle edge (the edge of the buttonhole stitch where the thread interlocks between one stitch and the next).

Diagram 16

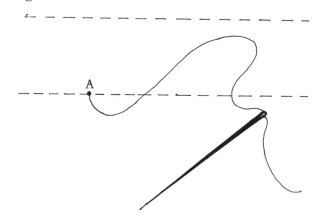

The needle is then inserted at B and re-emerges at C. Ensure that the loop of thread is under the needle.

Diagram 17

Continue stitching along the line in this manner as in diagram 18.

Buttonhole stitch uses a lot of thread so it is often necessary to replenish your supply. To do this so that the join will not be visible, do not finish off the old thread, but instead, insert it in your work above the completed stitch.

Diagram 18

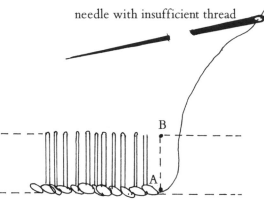

needle with insufficient thread

The new thread is secured on the wrong side by stitching it into the thread of the previous buttonhole stitches.

Bring the new thread through at A and recommence stitching.

Diagram 19

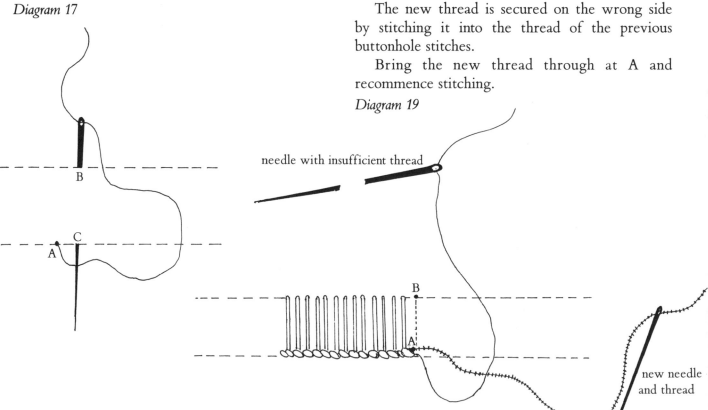

needle with insufficient thread

new needle and thread

Stitch for at least four or five more stitches before taking the old thread down at B and finishing off on the wrong side.

There are many variations of buttonhole stitch. They are very useful as borders and for embellishing seams in crazy patchwork (see Crazy Patchwork Cushion on page 139).

Examples of variations on open buttonhole stitches are given below.

Diagram 20

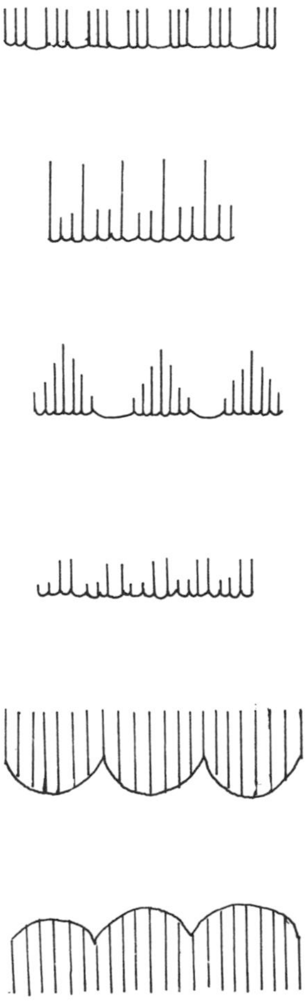

Diagram 21

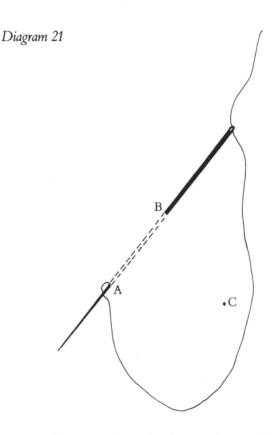

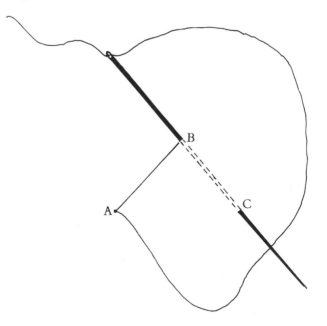

For the second stitch, insert the needle at B. This time, bring it out at C.

Diagram 22

Closed buttonhole stitch refers to the situation where buttonhole stitch is worked from the same hole for at least two stitches. This forms a triangular pattern.

The needle should be brought out at A and inserted at B; then it re-emerges at A.

Ensure that the thread is under the needle at A. Pull the needle through.

Make sure the thread is under the needle at C. Pull through. For the next stitch, the needle is inserted at D and re-emerges at C (see diagram 23).

Diagram 23

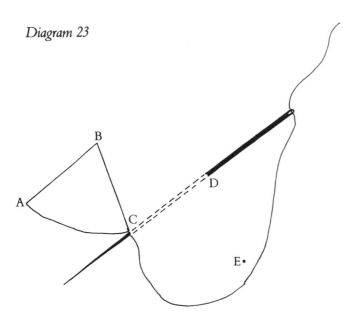

Continue stitching in this manner.

As with open buttonhole stitch, there are numerous variations with the closed type.

Diagram 24

Buttonhole stitch can be used very effectively to make flowers and leaves by creating circular shapes.

Diagram 25

For these shapes, always commence on the outside design line and stitch around.

To make the join invisible when stitching circular shapes, slip the needle under the first stitch as shown below.

Diagram 26

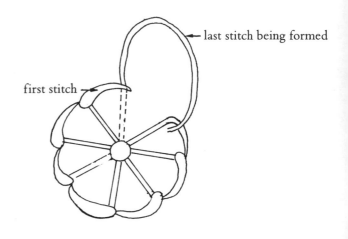

EYELETS

A. SMALL ROUND EYELETS

1. Mark position of eyelet with a dot.
2. Position the marked fabric in a screw-type embroidery hoop.
3. Make a small hole with a stiletto or awl.

Diagram 27

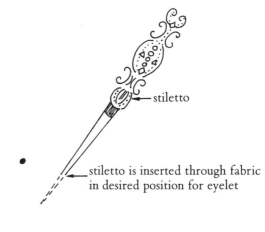

4. With a size 10 crewel needle and one strand of embroidery floss, stitch around the perimeter of the hole with small running stitches. Finish with the thread on the back of the fabric. Do not finish off thread.

Diagram 28

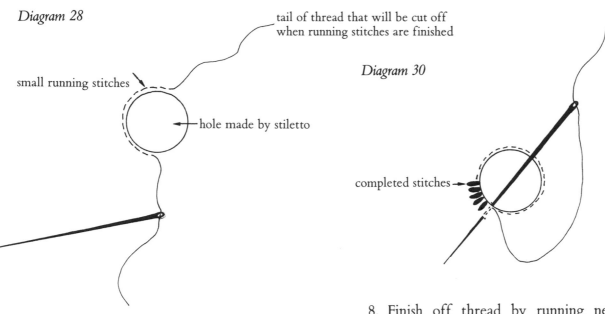

small running stitches

tail of thread that will be cut off when running stitches are finished

hole made by stiletto

5. Enlarge hole again with stiletto.

6. Bring the thread from the back of the fabric just outside running stitches and stitch from this point down into the hole, just beyond the outer perimeter of running stitches.

Diagram 29

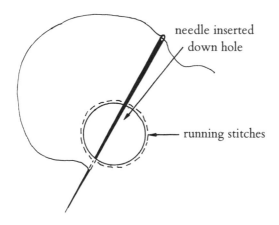

needle inserted down hole

running stitches

7. Continue in this manner until eyelet is complete.

Diagram 30

completed stitches

8. Finish off thread by running needle along completed stitch on the wrong side. Clip thread off close to the eyelet.

9. After stitching is complete, carefully re-insert the stiletto to slightly enlarge the eyelet.

B. LARGE ROUND OR OVAL EYELETS

This method is similar to that used for small eyelets. However, scissors must be used to make the hole in this instance. A stiletto will not provide a hole large enough for our purposes.

1. Mark position and outer perimeter of eyelet with a marking pen.

2. Outline outer perimeter with running stitches. Do not finish off the thread.

Diagram 31

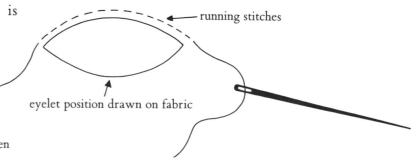

running stitches

eyelet position drawn on fabric

tail of thread to be cut off when running stitches are complete

3. Slit the centre of the eyelet with scissors.

Diagram 32

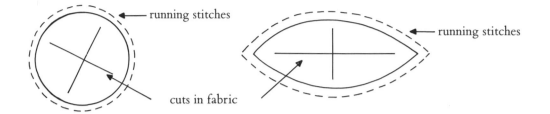

running stitches

running stitches

cuts in fabric

4. Fold excess fabric to the back of the work and finger press.

5. Bring needle from wrong side of fabric to right side just outside running stitches.

6. Stitch from this position by going down in the hole created and re-entering the fabric adjacent to the first stitch.

Diagram 33

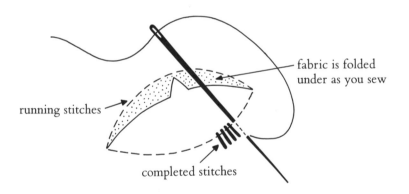

fabric is folded under as you sew

running stitches

completed stitches

7. Continue in this manner until eyelet is complete.

8. Finish off thread by weaving it into the wrong side of completed stitch.

9. Trim away excess fabric.

HADOWY FIGURES

Shadow work is based on one simple embroidery stitch, the double back stitch or closed herringbone. It is a very old technique and crude examples of it have been found dating back to the ancient Egyptians. Traditionally, shadow stitching was white on white but in its present form, myriad colours and many different fabrics can be used.

There are two methods of beginning shadow work:

1. The waste knot
2. The split stitch

1. WASTE KNOT

I consider this method too slow now, but as a beginner I used it a great deal.

1. Cut a piece of floss about 45 cm (18″) long and separate it into single strands.

2. Put a knot in one end and thread the other end through the needle.

3. Load your work into a hoop with the right side up. Pull fabric so that the working surface is fairly taut but the grain of the fabric is not distorted.

4. Bring the floss from the right side to the wrong side and make some large tacking stitches a little distance from your design.

5. Bring your floss from the wrong side to the right side on one of the design lines, at a point that we will call A.

6. Now you are ready to stitch. When stitching is complete or thread runs out, the tail with the knot is then re-threaded into the needle

Diagram 1

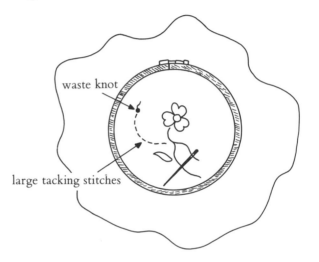

Diagram 2

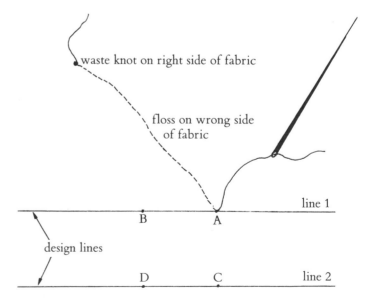

and woven into the back of the work to match completed stitching.

2. THE SPLIT STITCH

This is a much quicker method and does not require much practice.

1. Thread needle with one strand of floss.

2. Load work into a hoop so that the front side is up.

3. Bring the needle from the back of the work through to the front of the design at A. Leave about a 5 cm (2″) tail of thread on the wrong side.

Diagram 3

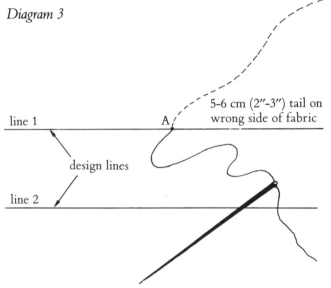

line 1   A   5-6 cm (2″-3″) tail on
                                           wrong side of fabric

            design lines

line 2

4. Take a back stitch from A to B, ensuring that the tail is held in place behind work.

5. Take a back stitch on line 2 between C and D, ensuring that, as the needle passes to E, it will pierce the floss tail.

Diagram 4

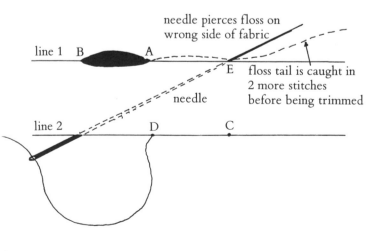

needle pierces floss on
wrong side of fabric

line 1   B   A
                      E   floss tail is caught in
                   needle   2 more stitches
                            before being trimmed

line 2   D   C

6. Pull so that thread on top lies flat.

7. As I embroider, I catch the tail in my work for a few more stitches before the excess thread is trimmed off.

FORMING DOUBLE BACK STITCH OR CLOSED HERRINGBONE

1. Secure the thread with the method of your choice.

2. Bring the needle from the wrong to the right side at A.

3. Take a back stitch from A to B on line 1. The needle goes down at B and re-emerges at C on Line 2.

Diagram 5

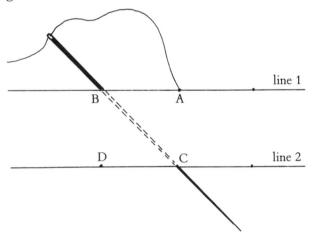

                                         line 1
        B   A

     D   C   line 2

4. Take a back stitch from C to D on line 2 and bring the needle out at E on line 1.

Diagram 6

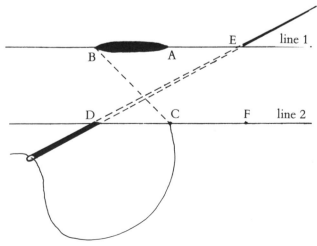

                            E   line 1
     B   A

     D   C   F   line 2

5. A back stitch is now taken between E and A and the needle enters the right side through F on line 2.

Diagram 7

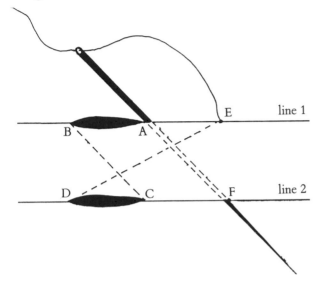

7. The third back stitch of line 1 is between G and E with the needle reappearing on line 2 at H.

Diagram 9

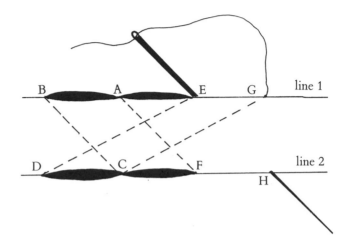

6. The second back stitch on line 2 is between F and C with the needle re-emerging at G on line 1.

Diagram 8

8. Stitching continues in this manner until the desired area is covered. A line of back stitches is formed on lines 1 and 2 with the thread areas crossed on the wrong side, giving a shadow of colour on the right side as in diagram 10.

Diagram 10

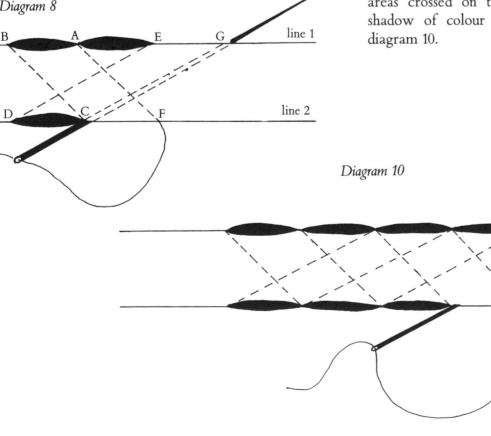

STITCH SIZE

Stitch length needs to be fairly short in order to:

1. Make curves smoother.

2. Obtain maximum concentration of colour on the back of the work. This is particularly important on heavier or less transparent fabrics.

A stitch of 1 to 2 mm (or a little less than $\frac{1}{16}''$) is ideal.

FINISHING OFF

Finishing off needs to be done carefully to ensure it is not visible from the right side.

If possible, it is best to finish off where stitches have converged, such as at a point where ribbons cross or where there is dense stitching at the centre of a flower.

Diagram 11

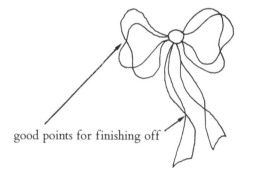

good points for finishing off

If it is possible to finish off at such a location, the thread can be darned into the previous stitches with no adverse effect on the appearance of the front. Try to organise your work so that starting and ending occur at such points.

On very transparent fabric, or where it is necessary to finish in an area where the stitches are not converging, follow this method.

At the point where you have finished stitching, take the thread to the wrong side of work (see diagram 12).

Diagram 12

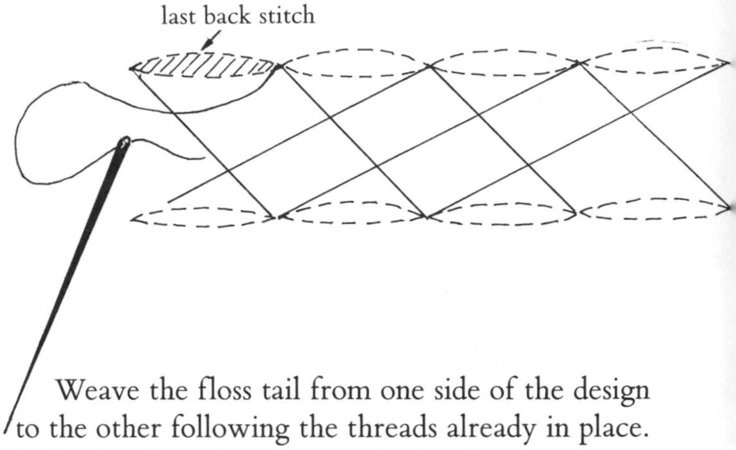

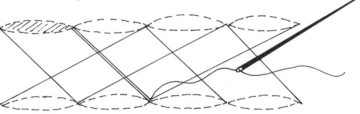

last back stitch

Weave the floss tail from one side of the design to the other following the threads already in place. Split the floss that is already in place to secure the weaving as you go. This weaving allows you to fill in any weak areas in the stitching where there is insufficient floss to give sufficient colour on the right side. This is of more importance when stitching irregular shapes such as the bluebirds on the bib (see Bluebird Bib, page 72).

Diagram 13

It is important to join the new thread in the correct position. The new thread must come from the same position as the old thread would have if it had not needed to be replaced. If this is not done there will be a gap in the thread as it passes across the back of your work and this will show on the front. To avoid this, weave the new thread in as shown in the diagram below.

Diagram 14

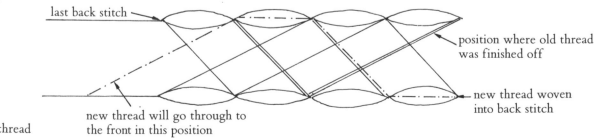

last back stitch

position where old thread was finished off

new thread woven into back stitch

new thread will go through to the front in this position

new thread

STITCHING AROUND A CURVE

On any curve, the inside curve has a smaller radius than the outside one. If stitching from the outside curve to the inside, a shorter stitch length is required on the inside curve and a longer one on the outside curve.

Diagram 15

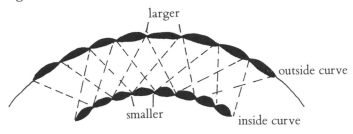

Achieving the correct balance between the two stitch sizes so that a satisfactory result is obtained is largely a matter of practice.

STITCHING OTHER SHAPES

The following diagrams set out suggestions for completing circles, hearts and other shapes.

Diagram 16

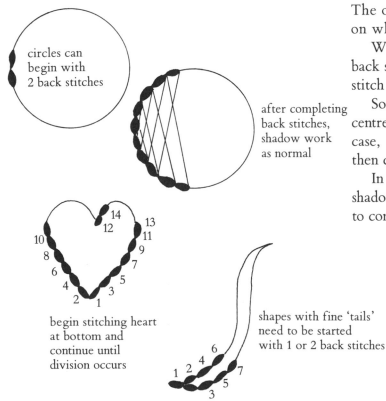

circles can begin with 2 back stitches

after completing back stitches, shadow work as normal

begin stitching heart at bottom and continue until division occurs

shapes with fine 'tails' need to be started with 1 or 2 back stitches

TOUCHING MOTIFS

In most designs there will be some points at which two motifs touch. There are two methods of dealing with this situation.

1. Double line of stitching (Stacking):
   The first motif is stitched as normal and finished off. The second motif is stitched, also as normal, but on the common areas there is a double line of stitching. It is important that the second motif's stitches use the same holes as the first. This method is most useful where it is desirable to add emphasis to a design line. It is often used where thread of the same colour is used in the second motif.

2. Underlacing:
   This method is used when a second row of stitching or 'stacking' is undesirable. The most prominent motif is stitched first. The second motif is stitched so that on the common design line the thread is caught in the threads of the previous stitch, rather than a back stitch being taken.

ORDER OF WORKING A DESIGN

The order in which you work a design depends on what are the dominant features.

Where there are shadow-worked leaves with back stitched veins, I would usually work the back stitch veins first, followed by the shadow work.

Sometimes satin stitch is used to highlight centres of shadow stitch flowers or bows. In that case, I prefer to do the shadow work first and then complete the satin stitch.

In the situation where there is a bouquet and shadow work is used in combination it is preferable to complete all the shadow stitching first.

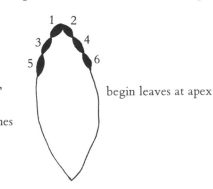

begin leaves at apex

OLDEN BULLION

Bullion stitch is very useful because it can be used to make a variety of flowers. It also washes and wears well. Many people consider it a difficult stitch, but if straw or milliner's needles are used, the process is made easier. Follow the instructions below and you will be stitching bullion flowers in no time.

BULLION STITCH

1. Bring the needle from the back of the fabric to the desired position to begin the first rose. The point where the needle enters the fabric is A.

Diagram 1

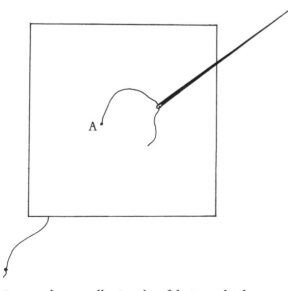

2. Insert the needle in the fabric a little more than 8 mm (¼″) above A. Bring it out again exactly through A. Do not pull thread right through and be careful not to split the floss as the needle passes through A.

Diagram 2

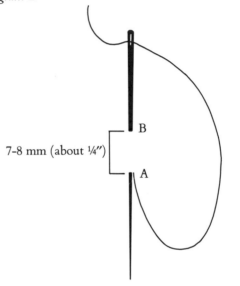

7-8 mm (about ¼″)

B

A

3. Move the work so that A is at the top and the needle is perpendicular to the floor.

Diagram 3

top half of needle exposed

A

B

fabric

4. If you are right-handed, hold the needle between your thumb and the middle finger of your right hand. Rest your index finger on the top of the exposed needle. The index finger will be used to control the tension and evenness of the winding process.

Wind the thread clockwise around the needle seven times; it must be firm but not extremely tight. Use your forefinger to keep the twists, or wraps, on the needle even, and to hold them down towards the fabric.

Diagram 4

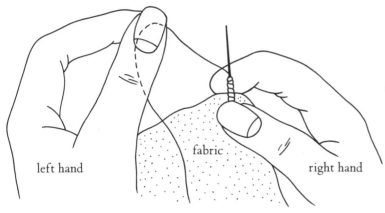

left hand   fabric   right hand

If you are left-handed, hold the needle in the same way as for right-handers, but in your left hand and wind the thread anti-clockwise.

5. Pinch the needle and wraps with the thumb and forefinger of your left hand (for right-handers) and pull needle through with your right hand. Left-handers will work the opposite way.

Diagram 5

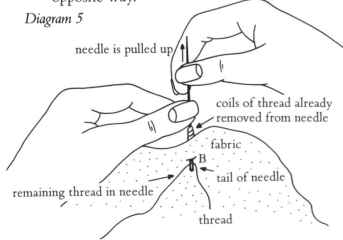

needle is pulled up

coils of thread already removed from needle

fabric

B

tail of needle

remaining thread in needle

thread

6. Now lay the work flat on a table, or your lap. Place the thread that is coming out of the top of the bullion between your thumb and index finger. Pull down to remove as much thread as possible from the bullion. Left-handers will work the opposite way.

Diagram 6

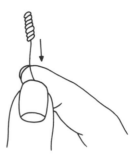

7. Check bullion to see that it looks even and that the twists are tight. If twisting is floppy, insufficient thread has been pulled out of the bullions, so repeat previous process.

Once you are happy with the bullion, insert the needle at B. This anchors the bullion stitch.

TO MAKE A ROUND BULLION ROSE
Round bullion roses consist of three rows of bullion stitch. The centre is made in the darkest shade of thread and the lightest is placed on the outside.

1. To begin the rose, use the darkest thread and make a back stitch of the desired length. Make one bullion with eight twists.

2. Still using the darkest thread, bring the needle out at a new position C. C is as close as possible to our original A without being in the same hole.

Diagram 7

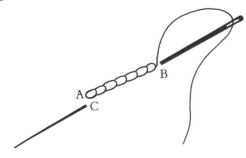

B
A
C

3. Pull the thread all the way through and, this time, insert the needle at D which is immediately adjacent to B; bring it out again at C. Repeat Steps 3 to 7 of the bullion stitch instructions to form another bullion.

Diagram 8

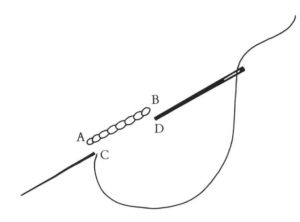

4. Repeat this process again so that there are three 8-twist bullions. After anchoring the last bullion, take the thread to the back and finish off by stitching into previous work.

5. Thread needle with medium shade. On the wrong side of the work, make a couple of back stitches into previous work to secure the thread.

6. Bring the needle through, near the bottom of the first bullion, and pull through.

Diagram 9

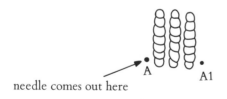

needle comes out here

7. For right-handers, re-insert the needle at the other side of the three bullions at B and come out again at A.

   Left-handers will come up at A1 and work a bullion between A1 and B1.

Diagram 10

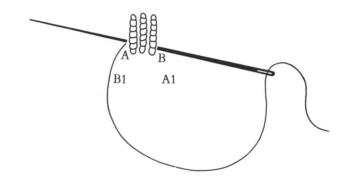

8. Make a bullion as before, this time using 10 twists. On this round, the bullions all overlap.

9. The second bullion in this row starts on the outside of the bullion just completed and halfway along it. All bullions in this row have 10 twists.

   If you are right-handed you will move around this row anti-clockwise as in diagram 11. If you are left-handed, work this row clockwise as in diagram 12.

Diagram 11 (for right-handers)

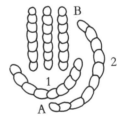

Diagram 12 (for left-handers)

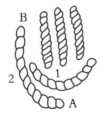

10. Complete four bullion stitches in this manner as shown below. The fourth bullion should finish so that there is a small space between it and the first (see diagram 13).

Diagram 13

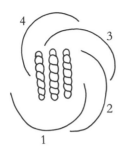

11. The fifth bullion will start on the outside of the fourth bullion and halfway along it. It will finish about halfway along the inside of the first bullion, as shown below. The thread for the fifth bullion will be wound onto the needle at A and secured at B (see diagram 14).

Diagram 14

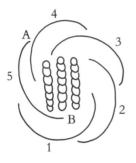

12. The thread may now be taken through to the back and finished off.

13. The final row can now be worked. Change to the lightest shade and complete in the same way as the second row, as follows.

14. Bring the needle out halfway along the outside of any bullion in the previous row. Now work a 12-twist bullion that extends halfway along the next bullion in the previous row.

15. When that is completed, bring the needle out on the outside of this bullion about halfway along; make another bullion (see diagram 15).

Diagram 15

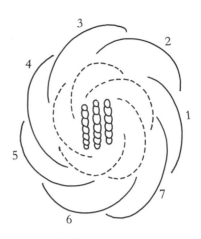

7th and final bullion finishes inside 1st bullion

16. Continue in this fashion until the final row is completed.

Remember that the final bullion is secured to the inside of the first. Take thread through to the back and finish off. This completes a round rose.

MAKING ROSES OF DIFFERENT SIZES

The following table is a guide to what needle size to use. It also gives the approximate size of the first bullion stitch when the number of strands of DMC floss is varied. It is intended *as a guide only* and you should always work a sample with the floss and the fabric that you have chosen to use.

Remember, the number of twists remains the same, only the size of the stitch for the initial bullion changes.

Number of strands of DMC floss	Needle sizes suitable	Length of initial stitch
6	3	7-8 mm (a little over ¼″)
5	4	7 mm (a little over ¼″)
4	5 or 6	6 mm (a little under ¼″)
3	6 or 7	5 mm (a little under ¼″)
2	8 or 9	4-5 mm (a little over ⅛″)
1	10	3-4 mm (a little under ⅛″)

LEAVES

Leaves are simply two 6-strand bullions with seven to 10 twists. The number of twists changes the size of the leaf. The two bullions share the same hole at the top and the bottom.

TINY BUDS

The buds are two 8-twist bullions worked close together. They are surrounded by two fly stitches in green.

1. Complete the bullions first.

2. Change to four strands of green thread and a No. 8 crewel needle.

3. Bring the needle out at A, above the completed bullion.

4. Take the thread around the bullion as shown in diagram 16.

5. Reinsert the needle in the fabric at B.

6. To anchor the fly stitch, the needle is then brought through at C as shown in diagram 16.

Diagram 16

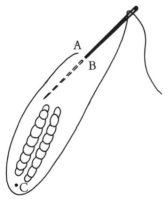

7. A small stitch is then taken over the thread already laid down by reinserting the needle in the fabric at D.

Diagram 17

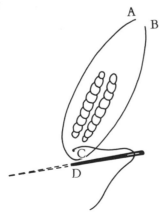

8. To complete the bud, another fly stitch is made with the needle entering at E adjacent to the first stitch but nearly level with the bullion. It finishes at F (see diagram 18).

9. The anchor stitch over this new thread must be completed as previously mentioned.

10. The stem is then completed in stem, outline or back stitch.

Diagram 18

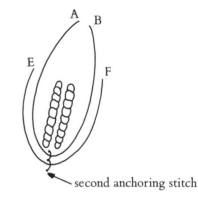

second anchoring stitch

SMALL BUDS

This produces a bud slightly larger than the one made by encasing the bullions in fly stitch.

1. Work one bullion with 10 twists; it is customary to work this in the darkest rose-coloured thread.

2. Work two 12-twist bullions in green, starting a very small distance from the top of the first bullion.

3. Anchor these bullions at the bottom in the same hole as the initial bullion stitch used.

Diagram 19

these bullions share the same hole at the bottom

MEDIUM BUDS

This is the largest of the buds; any larger and it would be a flower.

1. Begin as for the Small Bud (page 42), that is with one 10-twist bullion in the darkest rose colour.

2. Now work two 12-twist bullions on either side of the first, using the medium shade of floss in which the full flowers were worked. Make sure the second and third bullions start adjacent to the first, but are anchored at the bottom in the same hole.

Diagram 20

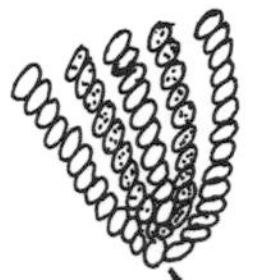

these bullions share the same hole at the bottom

3. Using the green thread, work two 14-twist bullions on either side. Start at the top adjacent to the previous bullion; at the bottom, move slightly under the position where the three other bullions are anchored.

Diagram 21

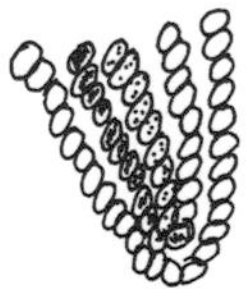

4. The two green bullions will share the same hole at the base of the bud.

SIDE-ON ROSES
These are excellent for adding variety to any bullion rose design.

1. Work three bullions with eight twists in the darkest shade, side by side, as you would for beginning a full-blown rose.

2. With the medium shade, work two bullions at the sides of these central three, using 10 twists per stitch.

Diagram 22

3. Now work a third stitch at the bottom to encase these two, also with 10 twists.

Diagram 23

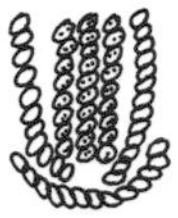

4. Change to the lightest shade and work four 12-twist bullions.

Diagram 24

DAISIES
Bullion daisies make wonderful flowers and are just as durable as bullion roses. The following method helps keep the flower even. Once completed, the centre can be filled with French knots.

1. When drawing the position of a daisy, I prefer to draw two concentric circles (like a doughnut), and only mark in four spokes of the daisy.

Diagram 25

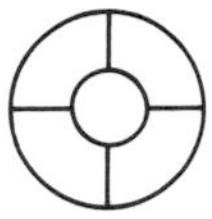

2. I work these four bullions first. I usually use 10-twist bullions, but this depends on the size of the flower and thread being used. It is always better to work a sample to check the desired effect before commencing the project.

3. After completing these four bullions, I then work the next four between those already completed (see diagram 26).

Diagram 26

4. Now go back and fill in the required number of bullions to fill in each space.

SIDE-ON DAISY

These are worked in much the same manner as the open daisy and are used to add variation to a design.

1. Draw design lines to resemble a section from a circle.

Diagram 27

2. Work three bullions, as indicated below, in the same number of twists that you are using for the full daisies.

Diagram 28

3. Now fill in the spaces between these three bullions. The top area is filled with French knots.

Diagram 29

French knots

FLAME FLOWER

A different flower, which can be used in almost any piece of work, is formed in the following manner.

This flower was used extensively in Sally's Gown (see page 141).

1. Using the darkest shade of thread, make four 10-twist bullions in the pattern shown below.

Diagram 30

2. Work a 12-twist bullion down the centre.

Diagram 31

3. In the lighter shade of thread, insert a bullion stitch between the central one and a stitch to one side of it. Usually a 14-twist bullion is required for this stitch.

Diagram 32

4. Repeat this on the other side, but finish this stitch slightly above the last one. This second stitch needs to be longer than the first so try a 16-twist bullion.

Diagram 33

5. To complete the flower a green, 10-twist bullion is placed around the base.

LOOPED FLOWERS

This is a lovely, textured flower that gives depth to your work. Although the bullions that comprise this flower are wrapped at least 35 times, this will not be a problem after you have mastered the basics of bullion stitch.

1. Begin by drawing a circle. The bullion will be worked between A and B. Wrap the bullion 35 times. Always work a sample; some threads may require many more wraps.

Diagram 34

2. The next stitch is between C and D. Make sure that the first bullion loop is under the needle when the second stitch is being wound.

Diagram 35

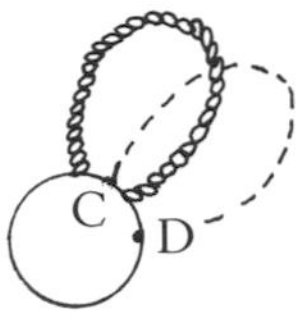

3. The next stitch will go between B and E. Continue in this fashion around the flower.

Diagram 36

4. The number of stitches required will vary according to the type of thread and the project itself. The last stitch will be as shown. (I like to tuck the anchor point for the last bullion under the first stitch.)

Diagram 37

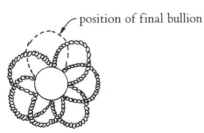

position of final bullion

FORGET-ME-NOTS AND SIMILAR FLOWERS

A beautiful forget-me-not can be made using bullion stitches. Don't limit this flower to blue; it looks fabulous in many other colours.

When working flowers with five petals, it is often difficult to get them evenly spaced around the centre. To overcome this, I use the '5 o'clock' rule.

Work the first petal at the 12 o'clock position and the next at the 5 o'clock position.

Diagram 38

Now one petal goes between the 12 and the 5 o'clock position on the right-hand side and two in the other space.

Diagram 39

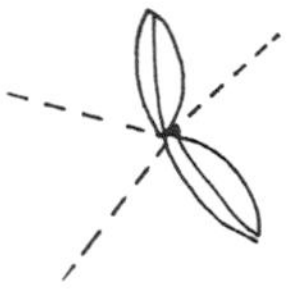

1. To make a bullion forget-me-not, work two bullion stitches, with approximately 10 twists, side by side. Make sure that they share the same holes at the top and the bottom. This forms one petal.

2. Complete five of these petals using the rule above.

3. Add a French knot, or perhaps a bead, to the centre and the flower is complete.

A great variation on this flower is used on one of the coat-hangers (see Coat-hanger Cover, Design 1, page 81).

1. In the darkest shade of floss, work one bullion stitch, using 10 wraps, to form each of five petals.

Diagram 40

2. Now change to a lighter floss and work two 12-wrap bullions around these first ones. Make sure that these new bullions share the same holes for the start and finish.

Diagram 41

3. Add a French knot, or a bead, to the centre to complete the flower.

LAVENDER

For the lavender, work the green stem first. The bullions are worked from the top of the stem down.

Diagram 42

bullion stitch with 10 twists

stem stitch

The bullion at the top of the stalk has 10 twists. As you proceed down the stem, gradually increase the number of twists on the bullions up to a maximum of 14 twists at the bottom of the stem.

Diagram 43

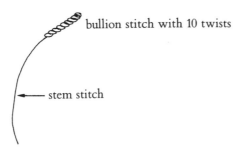

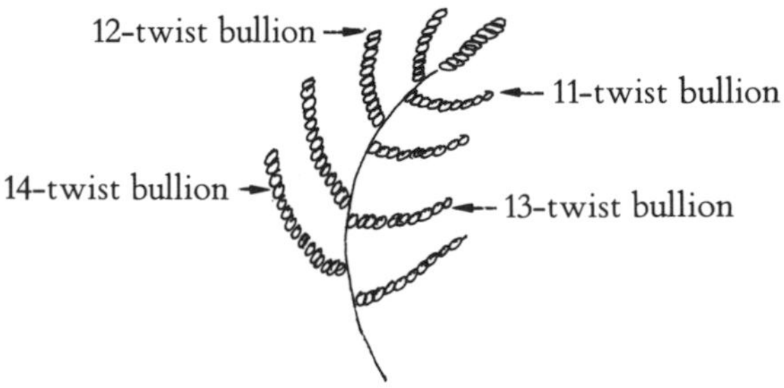

12-twist bullion →

← 11-twist bullion

14-twist bullion →

← 13-twist bullion

 MORE MAGIC

FRENCH KNOTS

French knots are easy to work and very useful in their application. If there are many to be worked in a design, it is best to use a hoop.

1. Bring the needle out at A.

2. Wrap the thread around the needle once.

   Sometimes it is suggested that more than one wrap be used to form a French knot. One wrap gives the knot a good, firm shape whereas more tend to fall over and look untidy. If a larger knot is required, try using a thicker thread and a larger needle.

Diagram 1

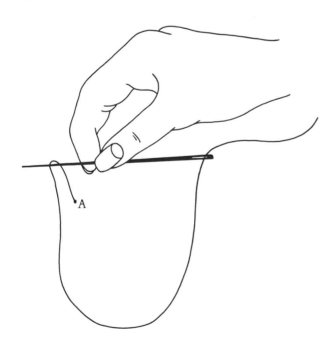

3. With the loop of thread around the needle, rotate the needle and insert it at a position very close to A, but not in the same hole as A.

Diagram 2

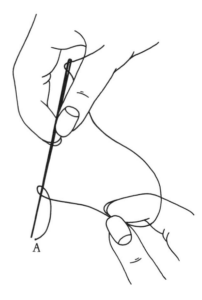

4. Pull on the excess thread firmly to tighten the knot on the needle (see diagram 3). When the knot is firm enough, push the needle through the fabric, ensuring it passes through the twisted thread. Finish off on wrong side of fabric by taking a couple of tiny back stitches.

Diagram 3

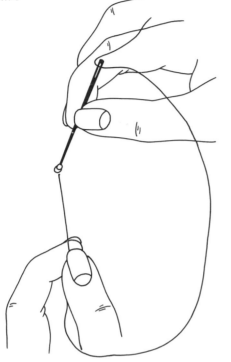

Insert the needle at B, making sure the thread is held taut while the needle is pushed through the fabric. Finish off on the wrong side or bring needle up in new starting position, as required.

Diagram 5

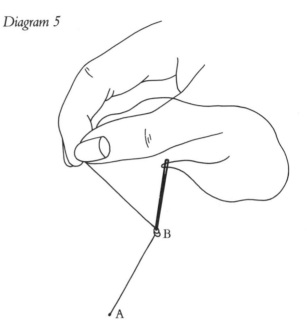

PISTAL STITCH

This is like a French knot, but with an extended tail.

1. Come up at A and pull the thread all the way through. Hold the thread at required length and wrap thread around the needle once.

Diagram 4

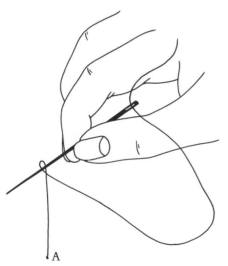

SINGLE CAST-ON STITCH

Cast-on stitch is an unusual one. It is very easy and can be a good alternative to bullion stitch in some circumstances.

1. Come up at A, down at B and up again at A. Be sure to leave your needle in the fabric.

Diagram 6

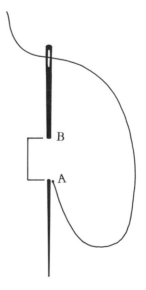

2. Loop the thread around your finger.

Diagram 7

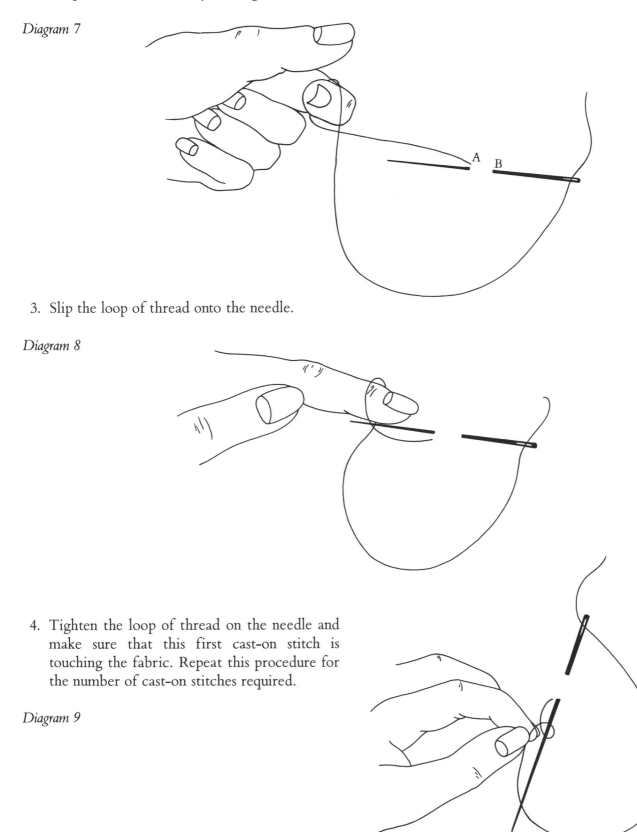

3. Slip the loop of thread onto the needle.

Diagram 8

4. Tighten the loop of thread on the needle and make sure that this first cast-on stitch is touching the fabric. Repeat this procedure for the number of cast-on stitches required.

Diagram 9

5. With your left hand, hold the cast-on stitches and pull the needle through them with your right hand.

Diagram 10

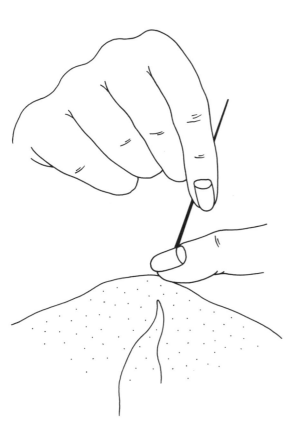

procedure as that for single cast-on stitch, cast on one loop on the needle, using the left-hand thread.

Diagram 11

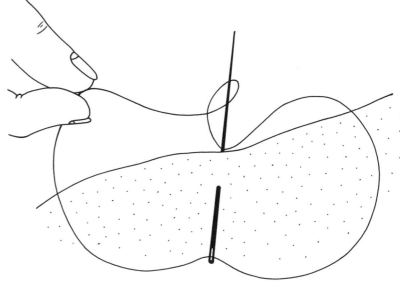

3. Now cast on one loop with the right-hand thread.

Diagram 12

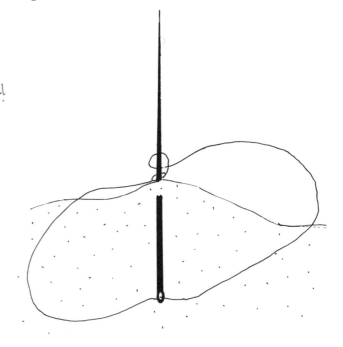

6. The cast-on stitch is anchored by pushing the needle down at or near the original B position.

DOUBLE CAST-ON STITCH

Double cast-on stitch gives a thicker result than single cast-on stitch; both edges are identical. For this stitch you must use a doubled thread that has its two ends knotted together.

1. As in single cast-on (see diagram 6, on page 48), come up at A, down at B and up again at A; leave the needle in the fabric.

2. Make sure one piece of the thread is on one side of the needle and the other piece is on the opposite side. Using the same casting-on

4. Continue to cast on stitches in this manner, remembering to alternate between left and right threads until the required number of loops are on the needle.

Diagram 13

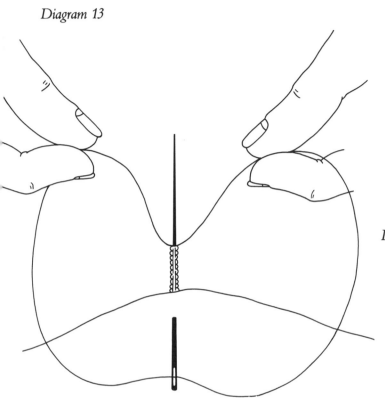

5. Before pulling thread through cast-on stitches, make sure the loops on the needle are not twisted. Using the same method as in step 5 of single cast-on stitch, pull the needle through all the loops.

6. Secure the stitch by taking needle to the wrong side of work just near the end of your stitch.

WHIPPED WEBS

This is a very easy embroidery stitch and is used extensively on the face washer and hand-towel designs (see page 86).

It is best to use a tapestry needle when weaving the web but it may be necessary to use a needle with a sharp point to lay down the spokes of the web.

1. Lay down the required number of spokes in straight stitch.

Diagram 1

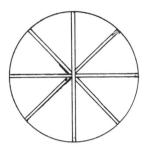

2. Bring needle up close to the centre at position 1 (between spokes A and B).

Diagram 2

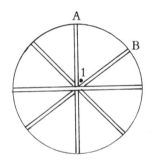

3. Go backwards over A and then forwards under spokes A and B (see diagram 3).

Diagram 3

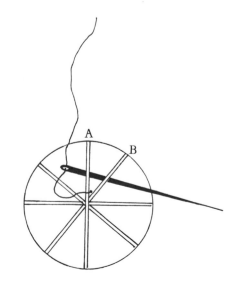

4. For the next stitch, go backwards over B and then forwards under the spokes B and C.

Diagram 4

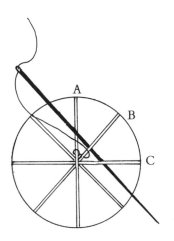

5. Continue around the web in this way until it is whipped the desired amount. It is important to pull the stitches firmly and to ease them towards the centre to produce a full, well-covered web.

ETTING IT TOGETHER

Once you have completed the embroidery, it is time to stitch the article together. Most construction work can be accomplished on the sewing machine. I have found that many of the techniques in heirloom sewing enhance embroidered articles.

Heirloom sewing is a sewing style that was popular from the early 1800s up until just before the first world war. Traditionally the garments made were sewn by hand, using the finest cotton fabric, and featured lace, puffing, embroidery and entredeux.

It is possible to duplicate this hand sewn look by using a sewing machine capable of zigzag stitch. For reference I have included my favourite heirloom techniques to aid your construction.

For all heirloom techniques, use fine machine threads such as Metler 60, DMC 50 or Tanne 80 and a size 60 machine needle. Ensure that your needle is in good condition.

HEIRLOOM SEWING TECHNIQUES

ROLL AND WHIP

This is the most basic technique and the result is excellent when done by machine.

Settings for roll and whip vary from machine to machine so it is essential to work a sample.

Set the sewing machine for a zigzag stitch and if possible 'de-centre' the needle to the maximum left position.

As a start, set the stitch length at 0.75 (or ¾) and stitch width at 3.

With the wrong side of the fabric up, place it under the presser foot.

Diagram 1

centre mark on presser foot

wrong side of fabric

fabric extends to the right of centre mark on presser foot

The needle must stitch through the fabric on the left and clear the fabric edge on the right in order to roll and whip.

Diagram 2

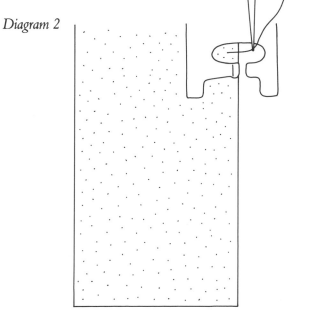

It is necessary to fine tune the settings on every machine. Once it is correct for your needs, make a sample and write the machine settings on the sample with a blue cloth marker. Iron this sample to make the writing permanent.

SEWING ENTREDEUX

Sometimes entredeux is stitched in its holes and other times we stitch in the 'ditch' beside the holes. To set your machine to sew the holes of the entredeux, use the following method.

Set machine to zigzag with needle position central. Initially set the stitch length at 1 and width at 3.

Using a small piece of entredeux, begin to stitch.

We need the machine to stitch in the holes of the entredeux, and then off into the batiste strip.

Diagram 3

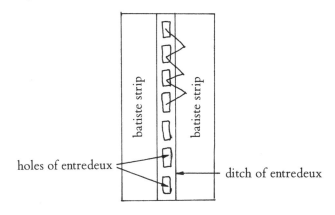

Once again, when you have established the appropriate settings for your machine, produce a sample and write the settings on it. These settings, particularly the stitch length, will be used repeatedly in heirloom sewing.

ATTACHING FABRIC TO ENTREDEUX

There are two methods that work well when applying entredeux to fabric. Which one I use depends on the situation. For example, I always use part of the 'stitch in the ditch' technique when attaching entredeux to collars but use the 'roll and whip' method when inserting Swiss insertions.

ROLL AND WHIP METHOD

1. Roll and whip the fabric edge according to the instructions on page 53. Press well.
2. Trim one side of the entredeux.
3. With right sides together, place the edges of the rolled and whipped fabric level with the edge of the entredeux.

Diagram 4

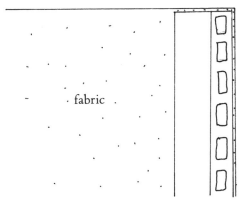

4. Using the settings found in Sewing Entredeux (this page), zigzag the entredeux and fabric together.

Diagram 5

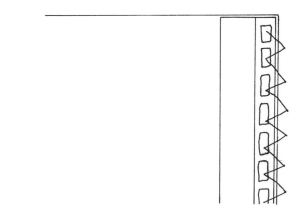

5. Turn to the right side and press.

STITCH IN THE DITCH METHOD

1. Cut off the required amount of entredeux, press. Do not trim.

2. With right sides together, and using a straight machine stitch such as length 1.5, stitch along the side of the entredeux holes.

Diagram 6

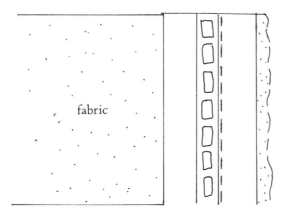

fabric

For some methods, such as making detachable collars, we stop at this point.

3. If we need to finish these raw edges, trim the batiste strip and the fabric to 3 mm (⅛″). Zigzag over the raw edge (see diagram 7). Some methods suggest zigzagging into the holes of the entredeux but this just complicates the technique with no benefit in appearance.

Diagram 7

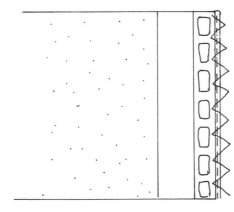

ROLL, WHIP AND GATHER

This is a very useful method for gathering large frills, as the finish is excellent and the gathering thread is strong and less likely to break.

1. Set your sewing machine with the same settings as for Roll and Whip (see page 53).

2. With wrong side of the fabric up, place it under the presser foot of the machine.

3. Lay quilting thread between where the needle will stitch on the left and the edge of the fabric.

Diagram 8

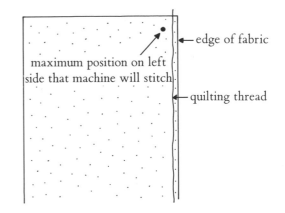

edge of fabric

maximum position on left side that machine will stitch

quilting thread

4. Roll and whip carefully. Be sure not to stitch through the quilting thread or it will be impossible to gather the fabric.

5. Pull the quilting thread from both ends to gather the fabric.

ATTACHING FLAT LACE TO ENTREDEUX

This works well when stitched by machine. You will find that the result is so good, you need never do it by hand. The technique used is known as the 'side by side' method of attaching flat lace to entredeux.

1. Trim one side of entredeux.

2. Butt the trimmed side of the entredeux to the edge of the lace.

3. Select the settings on your sewing machine used in Sewing Entredeux (see page 54), but note that the width of the stitch will depend on the width of the lace heading. It is advisable to do a sample for each project to get the best results.

Diagram 9

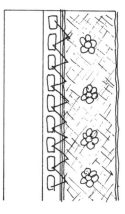

ATTACHING GATHERED LACE TO ENTREDEUX

Gathered lace can be attached to entredeux by machine, but personally, I like it better when done by hand. There are occasions, however, when time runs out and we are faced with the prospect of sewing it by machine or not sewing it at all. For these times I use the following method.

1. Gather the lace by pulling a thread in the heading.

2. Trim one side of the entredeux.

3. With right sides together, and the edges of the lace and entredeux even, zigzag in each hole of the entredeux. The machine settings used are those found in Sewing Entredeux (see page 54).

Diagram 10

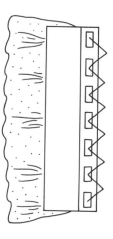

HAND WHIPPING GATHERED LACE TO ENTREDEUX

1. Gather lace the desired amount by pulling a thread in lace heading.

2. Trim one side of the entredeux.

3. With right side of the lace to right side of the entredeux, and the top edges even, whip over through each hole in the entredeux, picking up all the threads in the heading of the lace.

Diagram 11

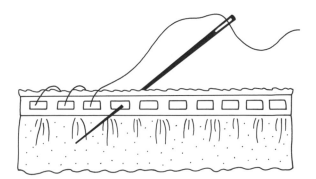

Gathers in the lace may be adjusted as you stitch. It is usually easier to have the entredeux facing you and the lace on the other side.

FABULOUS FASTENINGS

Buttons can be made a feature of any garment, especially if they match the embroidered item.

There are two great ways to add the embroidered touch to buttons:

1. By using a self-covering button with an embroidered motif.
2. By attaching the button with embroidery stitches.

SELF-COVER BUTTONS

MATERIALS

Self-cover buttons in the size required (the best sort are the kits that contain a button, a holder, a pusher and a button back. See diagram 1).
Embroidered motifs of choice
Small amount of additional fabric
Water soluble fabric glue, such as 'No more Pins'

Diagram 1

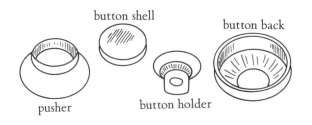

INSTRUCTIONS

1. When choosing an embroidery design for buttons, there are two things that it is important to consider:

   a. The design needs to be slightly smaller than the button.

   b. Non-directional designs are easier to handle in the covering process. This means that it is unnecessary to orientate the design relative to the button shank. It is possible to use directional designs but it is a bit more difficult. The extra effort in alignment is well worth it, though. For example, see the Bows and Redback Spider Projects (see pages 60 and 61).

2. Embroider motifs onto 10 cm x 10 cm (4" x 4") pieces of fabric. I usually draw up squares on fabric, complete the embroidery, then wash and iron the fabric before any of the squares are cut out. Remember to do a few extra embroidered squares. This gives you a few to practice on and a spare button to sew onto the completed garment.

3. If you are using a very fine fabric such as voile, it may be necessary to back each embroidered square with another layer of fabric to prevent the button shell showing through. Two methods work well:

   i. A fine, double-sided fusible web, such as Wonder Under, can be applied to the wrong side of the embroidered square. The backing is then peeled away and the additional piece of fabric fused to the exposed surface. Follow the manufacturer's instructions for these fusible webs. Remember: if the embroidery is raised, make sure it is placed with the right side down into a thick towel when ironing or applying the web.

ii. Water-soluble glue is applied around the edges of the square and allowed to dry, bonding the two pieces of fabric sufficiently to permit the button to be covered. I have tried applying fusible interfacing to the back of the embroidered square instead of the self fabric, but this is not very successful. No matter how lightweight it is, it stiffens the fabric and this makes getting a smooth edge around the button almost impossible. It is a good idea to make a test sample of a button just using the fabric without the embroidery to see if two layers are necessary. It is always easier to cover buttons with a single layer of fabric but, if this gives a poor result, it is well worth the additional effort of using a double layer.

4. Hold the button holder so it is orientated like a cup and then place the right side of the embroidery face down over it. Place the button shell on top of this with the convex side facing the bottom of the 'cup'. Push the button shell to the bottom of the cup.

Diagram 2

5. Now turn the button holder over and check that the embroidery design is centred. It may be necessary to adjust the fabric or to redo step 4.

Diagram 3

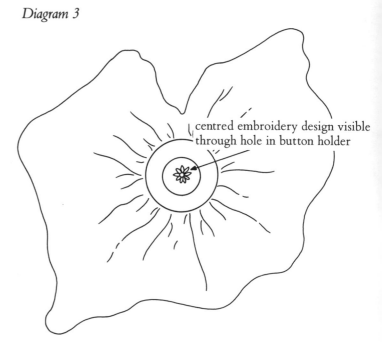

centred embroidery design visible through hole in button holder

6. Trim the excess fabric away from the rim of the button holder. Leave approximately 6 mm (¼″) of fabric extending from the rim of the button holder.

Diagram 4

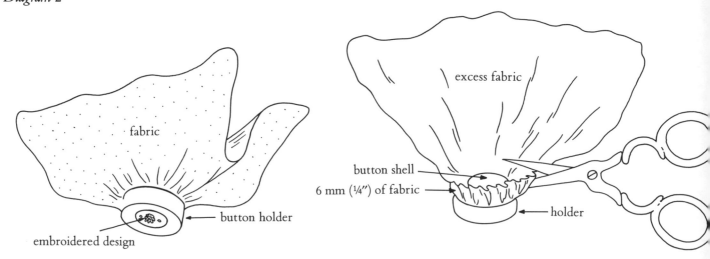

fabric

button holder

embroidered design

excess fabric

button shell

6 mm (¼″) of fabric

holder

7. Add a small amount of water-soluble fabric glue to the concave side of the button shell.

Diagram 5

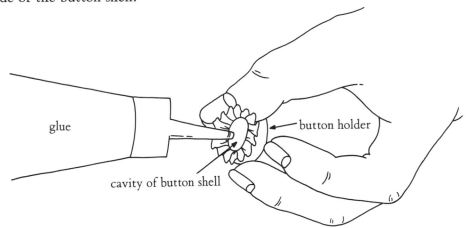

8. Using a sharp object (I use an old pair of embroidery scissors), tuck the excess fabric into the concave side of the button shell (see diagram 6).

Diagram 6

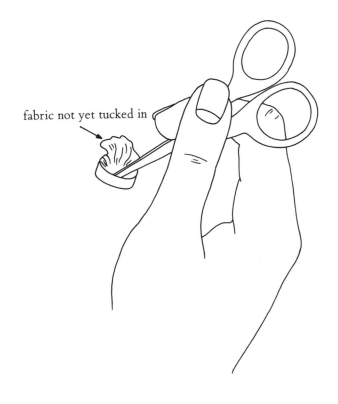

Diagram 7

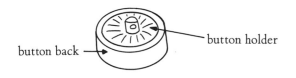

10. Take the pusher and insert it in the holder. Apply firm pressure to complete the button.

Diagram 8

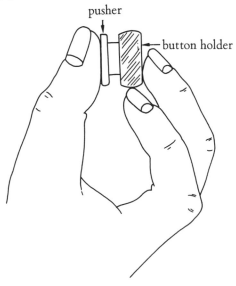

9. Place the button back into the holder with the shank uppermost (see diagram 7).

11. Remove the completed button from the shell.

EMBROIDERED BUTTONS

1. BOWS

MATERIALS

Remnant of calico (muslin)
Remnant of navy fabric (I used Capitol Imports navy handkerchief linen)
Madeira silk floss in 1007 (navy) and 306 (cream)
Size 10 straw needle
19 mm (¾″) self-cover buttons (in number required)

INSTRUCTIONS

The bows were worked on 10 cm (4″) squares of fabric.

All embroidery was done in one strand of floss.

Trace the bows onto the fabric.

The tails of the bows were worked first. They consisted of two 40-twist bullions.

The loops were also two bullions, but with 45 wraps per stitch.

Diagram 1

2. RED FLOWER

MATERIALS

Remnant of navy fabric
19 mm (¾″) self-cover buttons (in number required)
Madeira silk floss in 210 (red) and 114 (yellow)
Size 10 and size 7 straw needles

INSTRUCTIONS

Trace the flower outline onto the fabric, being sure to mark the quarter positions on the circle.

The petals are in Madeira 210 and are 36-twist bullions. There are eight overlapping bullions per flower.

Begin working bullions as shown in the diagram.

Diagram 2

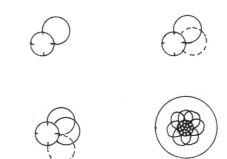

Continue in this fashion until all eight bullions are complete.

The centres are one-wrap French knots in two strands of Madeira 114.

Fill in the centre so no navy fabric shows through.

3. REDBACK SPIDERS

MATERIALS

Remnant of calico (muslin)
23 mm (1″) self-cover buttons
Madeira floss in 210 (red) and 1007 (navy)
Size 10 straw needle
Size 10 crewel needle

INSTRUCTIONS

All embroidery is in one strand of floss.

Trace spiders onto fabric.

Diagram 3

The following diagram shows the arrangement and number of twists per bullion required to make the spider.

Diagram 4

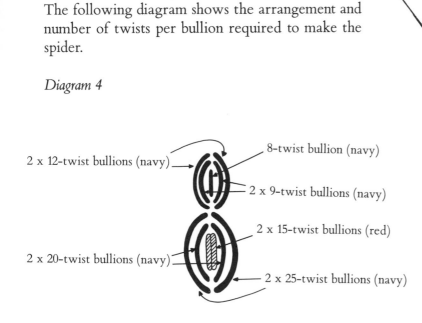

2 x 12-twist bullions (navy)
8-twist bullion (navy)
2 x 9-twist bullions (navy)
2 x 15-twist bullions (red)
2 x 20-twist bullions (navy)
2 x 25-twist bullions (navy)

The legs of the spider are worked in bullion stitch.

ATTACHING BUTTONS WITH BULLION STITCH

MATERIALS

Size 10 straw needle
Single strands of embroidery floss in colours of choice
Required number of buttons with 4 holes in them

1. Bring the needle through from the back of fabric to the desired position for attaching the

button. The point where the needle enters the fabric will be known as A.

Diagram 1

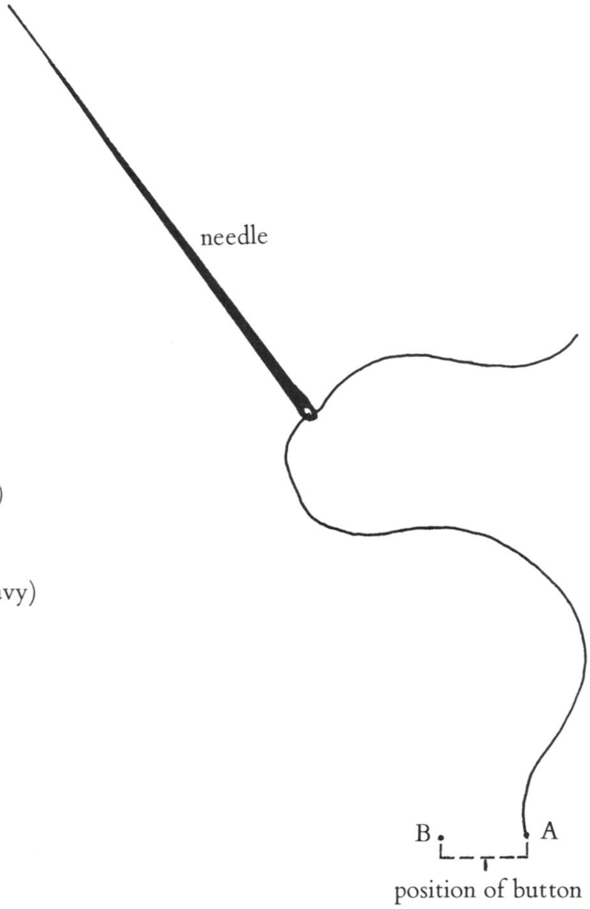

needle

B ● ⌐ ⌐ ● A
position of button

2. Thread the button onto the embroidery floss by coming up from underneath the button and going down in another hole of the button. The positon of this floss will be the position of the bullion. It is essential to leave a large loop of thread between A and where the button is threaded onto the floss (see diagram 2). The needle will re-enter the fabric at B. The distance between A and B is approximately the same distance between the hole in the button. The needle will re-emerge at A. The needle needs to be left in the fabric so the bullion can be wound.

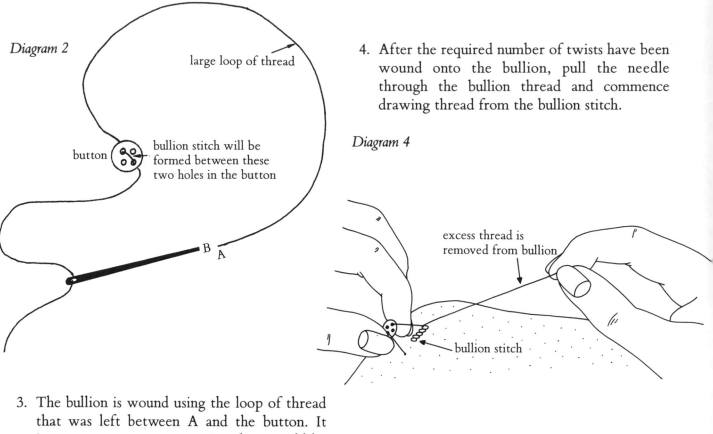

Diagram 2

large loop of thread

button

bullion stitch will be formed between these two holes in the button

B ‾ A

4. After the required number of twists have been wound onto the bullion, pull the needle through the bullion thread and commence drawing thread from the bullion stitch.

Diagram 4

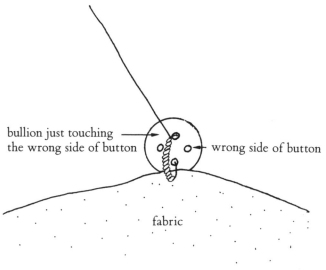

excess thread is removed from bullion

bullion stitch

3. The bullion is wound using the loop of thread that was left between A and the button. It is necessary to use more twists than would be necessary to cover the distance from A to B as the bullion needs to travel up the button, across it and down again. For a button 10 mm (½″) in diameter with holes 1 mm (¹⁄₂₅″) apart, 20 twists were necessary.

5. Continue pulling thread out until the bullion stitch just touches the wrong side of the button (see diagram 5).

Diagram 5

bullion just touching the wrong side of button

wrong side of button

fabric

Diagram 3

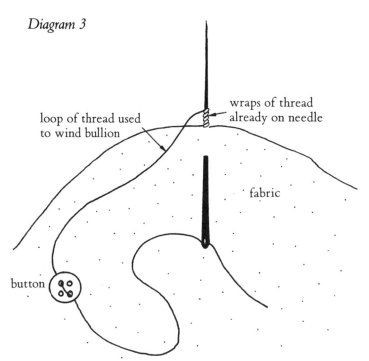

wraps of thread already on needle

loop of thread used to wind bullion

fabric

button

6. Insert the needle through the hole in the button immediately adjacent to the bullion stitch (see diagram 6).

Diagram 6

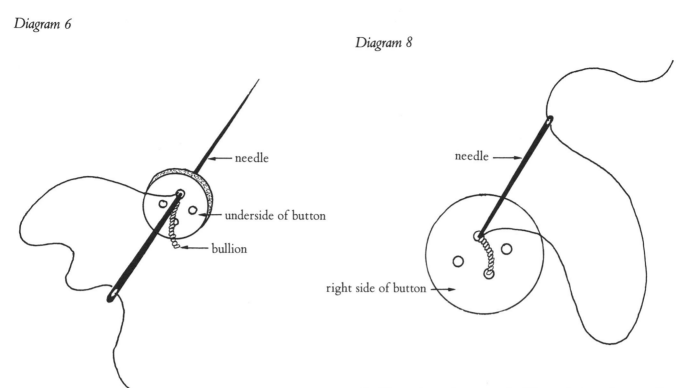

7. Ease the bullion stitch through the buttonhole by gently pulling upwards.

Diagram 7

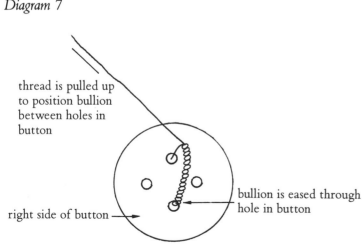

thread is pulled up to position bullion between holes in button

right side of button

bullion is eased through hole in button

8. When the bullion is positioned satisfactorily, insert the needle through the second hole in the button as shown in diagram 8.

Diagram 8

needle

right side of button

9. To make subsequent bullions, bring the needle out under the button adjacent to the initial position A.

Diagram 9

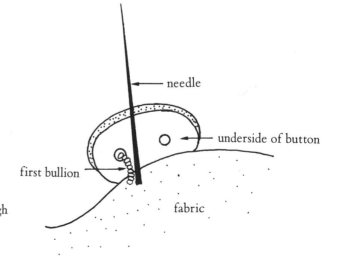

needle

underside of button

first bullion

fabric

10. Insert the needle carefully through the hole that already contains the first bullion. Make sure that none of the previous bullion is caught in this new stitch. It is necessary to leave a large loop of thread when the needle is pulled through the first hole (see diagram 10).

Diagram 10

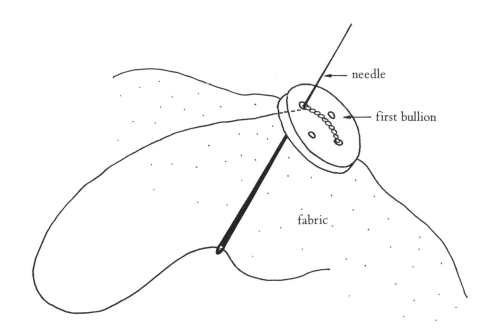

needle

first bullion

fabric

11. Hold the loop of thread with your thumb to prevent it being pulled through. Insert the needle into the second hole. Leave the needle in the fabric.

Diagram 11

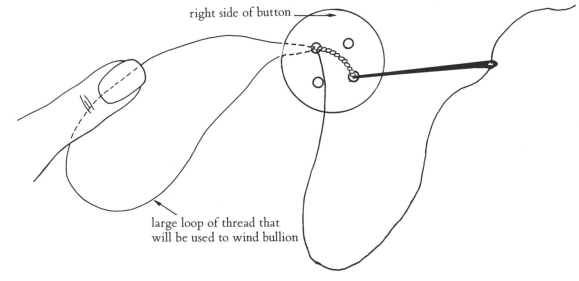

right side of button

large loop of thread that will be used to wind bullion

12. Reinsert the point of the needle (its shaft is still inserted in the second hole in the button) so it comes through the fabric at the point at which the thread is coming out adjacent to position A as shown in diagram 12.

Diagram 12

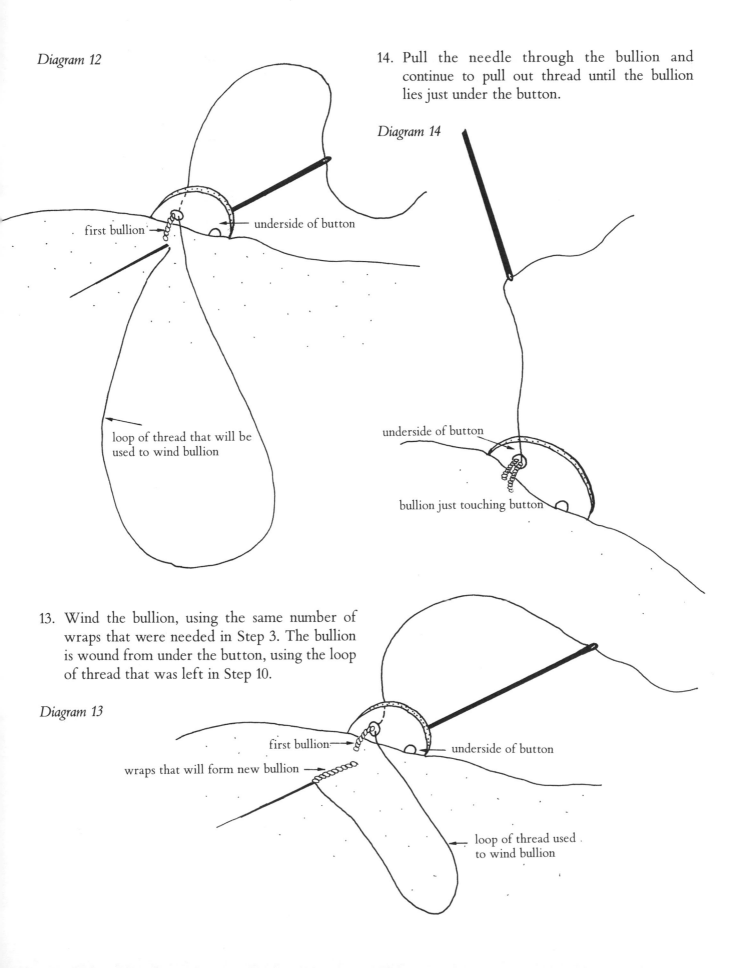

14. Pull the needle through the bullion and continue to pull out thread until the bullion lies just under the button.

Diagram 14

first bullion

underside of button

loop of thread that will be used to wind bullion

underside of button

bullion just touching button

13. Wind the bullion, using the same number of wraps that were needed in Step 3. The bullion is wound from under the button, using the loop of thread that was left in Step 10.

Diagram 13

first bullion

underside of button

wraps that will form new bullion

loop of thread used to wind bullion

15. Reinsert the needle through the hole in the button.

Diagram 15

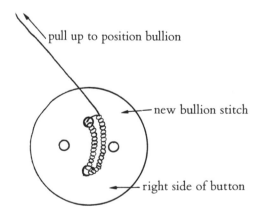

16. Gently pull the bullion stitch through the hole and settle it next to the previous bullion.

Diagram 16

17. Insert the needle in the second hole to anchor the bullion (see diagram 17).

Diagram 17

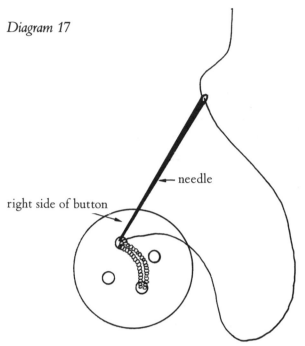

Repeat steps 9–17 if another bullion stitch is required.

When the desired number of bullions has been completed finish off thread by darning into work behind the button. Three bullions per each hole in the button is usually the upper limit.

LAZY DAISY LEAVES

NOTE: A size 10 straw needle is used for this stitch because of its fineness and length.

1. Thread a size 10 straw needle with one strand of green floss. Fasten the thread behind the button before bringing it through the desired hole in button.

Diagram 1

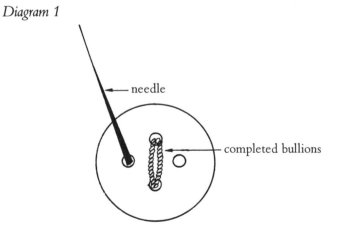

2. Reinsert the needle in the same hole in the button, being sure to leave a large enough loop of thread with which to work. It will take practice to determine the length required.

Diagram 2

4. Pull needle through loop and continue tightening thread until lazy daisy stitch has the desired look.

Diagram 4

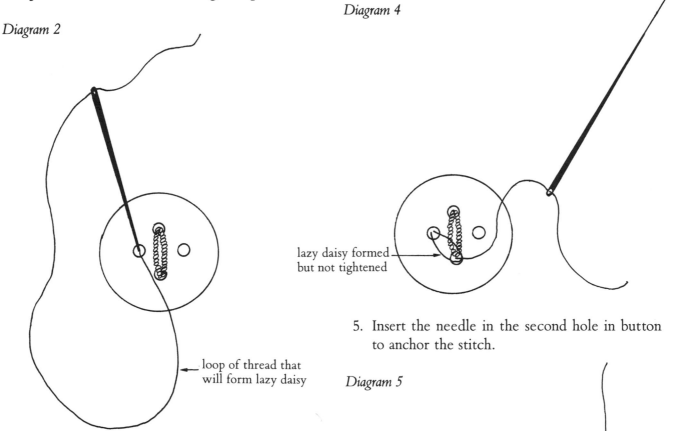

lazy daisy formed but not tightened

loop of thread that will form lazy daisy

5. Insert the needle in the second hole in button to anchor the stitch.

Diagram 5

3. Pull needle through, cnsuring the loop of thread remains on the top of the button. Bring needle from the wrong side through the second hole in button so that it catches the loop of thread. Be careful not to catch any of the bullion stitches.

Diagram 3

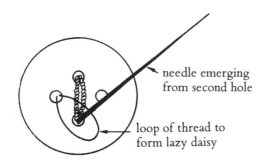

needle emerging from second hole

loop of thread to form lazy daisy

lazy daisy in desired position

Repeat for other leaf.

At the completion of two lazy daisy stitches, fasten off behind button.

ANDKERCHIEFS

MATERIALS

30 cm x 30 cm (12″ x 12″) piece of fine fabric such as handkerchief linen, voile or batiste

1.4 m (1½ yd) entredeux

1.7 m (2 yd) lace edging

In the samples, the Capitol Imports edgings used are:

Design 1: 1985 (wide lace edging)

Design 2: 770 (medium width edging)

Design 3: 2649 (narrowest edging)

Fine cotton to match fabric

DMC floss for embroidery:

Designs 1 and 2 use DMC 962 Medium pink and 523 Light green

Design 3 uses DMC 961 Dark pink, 962 Medium pink, 3326 Light pink and 523 Light green

EMBROIDERY INSTRUCTIONS

Trace design in an appropriate position on the fabric so that, once embroidered, the handkerchief can be cut out and finished off.

All shadow work, eyelets, back stitch and stem stitch require a size 10 crewel needle. The bullion stitch requires a size 10 straw needle. The French knot centres are stitched with a size 7 straw needle.

DESIGN 1

The petals of the flowers are shadow worked in one strand of DMC 962. The centres are French knots in two strands of DMC 962.

The leaves are shadow worked in DMC 523 and the stems are back stitched in the same thread.

Design 1   **Actual size**

DESIGN 2

The petals are shadow stitched in DMC 962 and the centres are eyelets in the same thread.

The leaves and stems are in DMC 523. All leaves are in shadow work and stems are back stitch.

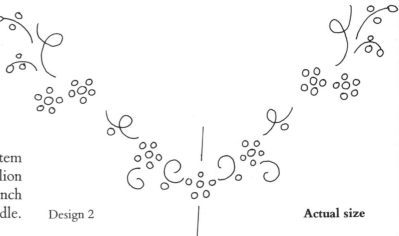

Design 2   **Actual size**

DESIGN 3

The centres of the roses are in one strand of DMC 961 and consist of three bullions with eight twists per stitch.

The first round of the roses is in DMC 962; there are 10 twists per bullion.

The final round is in DMC 3326; there are 12 twists per bullion.

The leaves consist of two bullions with eight twists in DMC 523.

The stems are stitched in stem stitch in DMC 523.

The large buds consist of one bullion with eight twists in DMC 961, two bullions also with eight twists in DMC 962 encased by two 10-twist bullions in DMC 523.

The small buds are made of one bullion with eight twists in DMC 961. This is enclosed by two 10-twist bullions in DMC 523.

The bows are worked in shadow work, using one strand of DMC 962.

Design 3   **Actual size**

HANDKERCHIEF CONSTRUCTION

1. Position the embroidery design appropriately and then, by pulling threads, cut a piece of fabric 30 cm x 30 cm (12″ x 12″).

2. Press and lightly spray starch.

3. Using the sewing machine, roll and whip all four edges of the fabric square.

4. Press well. Finish off thread tails by hand-stitching into the rolled and whipped hem.

5. Cut four pieces of entredeux 35 cm (14″) long. If using a different-sized square of fabric,

ensure that each strip of entredeux is 4–5 cm (1½″-2″) longer than the length of the side of the fabric.

6. Trim one side of each of the four pieces of entredeux. Press.

7. Trim 3–4 cm (1″-1½″) of the batiste strip from each end of one strip of entredeux.

Diagram 1

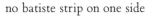
no batiste strip on one side

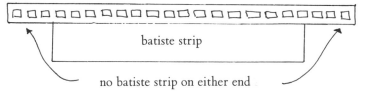
batiste strip

no batiste strip on either end

8. With rights sides together, zigzag entredeux to one side of the fabric.

Diagram 2

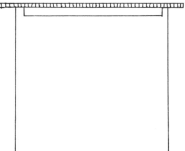

9. Turn to the right side and press. Do not cut off excess sewing thread; this will be used later.

10. Take a second piece of entredeux and trim 3–4 cm (1″-1½″) off the batiste strip as in step 7.

11. With right sides together, and ensuring that the trimmed areas of the two pieces of entredeux overlap, zigzag the second piece of entredeux to fabric. It is important that your stitching does not begin until you are on the fabric. We do not want to join the two pieces of entredeux together at this stage. See diagram 3.

Diagram 3

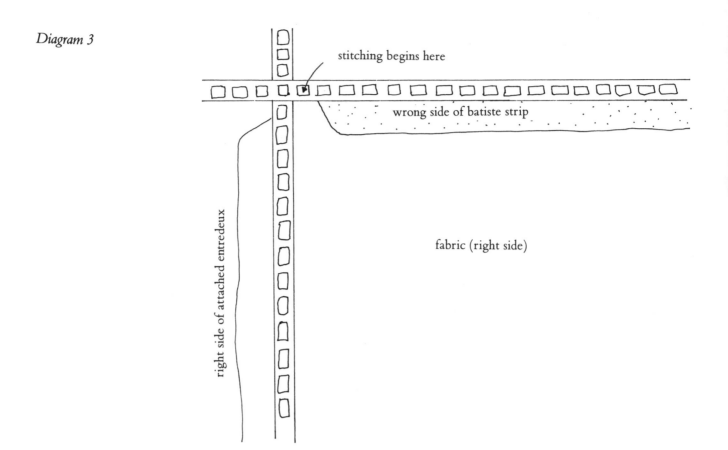

stitching begins here

wrong side of batiste strip

right side of attached entredeux

fabric (right side)

12. Turn the fabric to the right side and press well.
    The fabric square should look like the diagram
    below.

Diagram 4

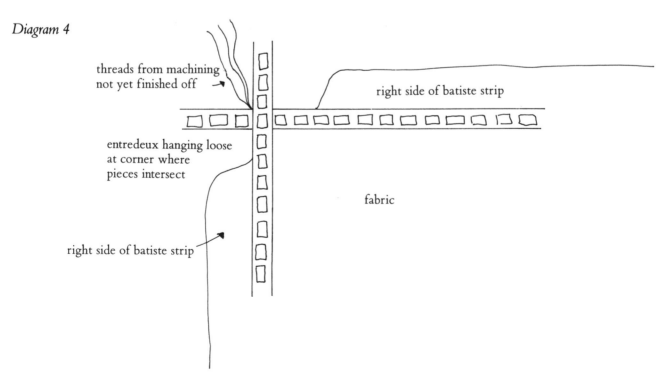

threads from machining
not yet finished off

right side of batiste strip

entredeux hanging loose
at corner where
pieces intersect

fabric

right side of batiste strip

13. Repeat steps 9 to 12 for the other two pieces of entredeux.

14. After all the entredeux has been attached, trim all the remaining batiste strips from the entredeux. Press.

15. Using a handsewing needle (a size 9 crewel needle is a good choice), thread one strand of the excess thread that is at the corner and carefully stitch the two intersecting pieces of entredeux together. Trim the entredeux to form a neat corner.

16. Finish off the other remaining threads at that corner by darning them into the fabric.

17. Repeat steps 15 and 16 for the other three corners. Press well.

18. For handkerchiefs, I prefer simply to gather the lace slightly where it goes around the corner rather than mitre it.

    Take lace edging, but do not gather it at this point. Be sure to leave about a 7-10 cm (3"-4") tail of lace before your begin stitching. Using the side-by-side method of attaching lace to entredeux (see pages 55-6), and beginning about four entredeux holes from the corner, commence zigzagging lace to handkerchief. See diagram 5.

19. Stop stitching about four entredeux holes from the next corner. Leave your machine needle in the down position in a hole of the entredeux.

20. On the lace heading, about 12 cm (5") from where you have stopped stitching, pull a thread in the heading of the lace to form some gathers. Using a small screw-driver, gently push the gathers back to the corner so that the lace is eased satisfactorily around the corner. Zigzag in position. The excess thread from the lace has been sewn into position.

21. Continue applying lace in this fashion until you reach the last corner. Gather the lace as if you intend to turn the corner, but stop stitching at the corner hole (where the two pieces of entredeux cross). Remove work from sewing machine.

22. Thread the excess cotton from the machine stitching into a handsewing needle and complete joining the lace to the entredeux by hand. Mitre lace at the corner with handstitching. Finish off all other loose threads by darning them in.

23. Trim excess lace from the mitre and overcast seam by hand, if desired. Trim any other excess threads from the handkerchief. Press well.

Diagram 5

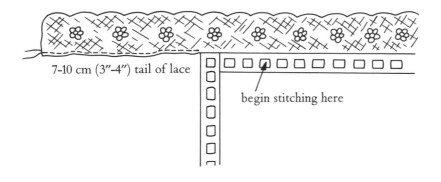

7-10 cm (3"-4") tail of lace

begin stitching here

BLUEBIRD BIB

Christenings are always special times for families. Often, the baby wears an heirloom christening gown that has been handed down for generations. This is a wonderful tradition, but I always feel that there should be some special piece of clothing that is kept for each individual child, as a memento. If you feel this way, why not make a beautiful hand-embroidered bib? As well as being a keepsake, this bib will also offer some much-needed protection to the treasured family heir-loom. Embroidered bibs launder well.

MATERIALS

36 cm (14") x 115 cm (45") wide batiste
Towelling remnant 36 cm x 36 cm (14" x 14")
1 m (40") white entredeux
2 m (80") Capitol Imports lace edging 2026
DMC floss:
  353 Apricot, 341 Light blue, 368 Light green
Bias strip 4-5 cm (1¾") x 25 cm (10"). There is sufficient batiste fabric to cut this bias strip
For neck tie, 50 cm (20") white ribbon 20 mm (¾") wide

Optional:
For rosettes, 4 m (4½ yd) white ribbon 1.5 mm (1/16") wide
White quilting thread

INSTRUCTIONS

1. Embroider bib. All embroidery is worked in one strand of floss using a crewel needle. Shadow stitch is used for the flowers and the bluebirds (which are both worked in DMC 341), as well as the ribbon which is in DMC 353. Back stitch in DMC 368 completes the stems.

2. Cut one bib from embroidered fabric.
   Cut two bibs from plain fabric.
   Cut one bib from towelling.

3. Trim batiste strip from one side of entredeux. Clip into strip on the other side. Press.

4. With right sides together, pin entredeux around embroidered bib using 8 mm (¼") seam allowance.

5. Stitch in the ditch (see page 55) of entredeux. Press.

6. With right sides together, place one of the plain fabric bibs on top of the embroidered bib. Pin.

7. Using the previous stitching line as a guide, stitch the two bibs together.

8. Clip and trim seam.

9. Turn to right side and press well.

10. With right sides together, join the towelling bib piece to the remaining batiste bib. Trim seams, turn through to the front and press well.

11. Place the embroidered bib (with the embroidery facing upwards) on top of the towelling bib. The back of the embroidered bib should lie on top of the batiste front of the towelling bib.

12. Pin the two sets of bibs together around the neck edge. (I usually machine-baste the bibs together at this stage to make handling easier.) To machine-baste, run a line of machine

Design for Bluebird Bib

Actual size

stitching around the neck edge 3 mm (⅛″) from the edge.

13. Fold the bias strip in half lengthways and mark the centre.

14. From this centre position, curve the folded bias strip in the shape of the neckline. Press.

15. Pin the raw edge of the folded bias strip to the raw edge of the bib neckline, being sure to match the centres. Some of the bias strip will hang over the edge of the bib on both sides.

16. Machine stitch, starting at the neck edge around the neckline area. Trim the seam slightly on the neck edge and clip curve.

17. On the neck edge, fold the bias strip to the back of the bib. Pin in position. At this stage, it will be necessary to trim the ends of the bias strip so they can be tucked in to give a neat finish on the neckline.

18. Either hand-whip the bias strip in position or sew through all thicknesses with a straight stitch on the sewing machine. Press.

19. Gather lace and apply to entredeux by either hand or machine.

20. Handstitch 20 mm (¾″) ribbon in position on each side of the neck. I usually do not cut this ribbon to length until it can be fitted on the baby.

Actual size

KNOTTED RIBBON ROSETTES

INSTRUCTIONS

1. Each rosette is made from 2 m (2¼ yd) ribbon 1.5 mm (¹⁄₁₆″) wide.

2. Make a knot every 2.5 cm (1″) along the length of the ribbon.

3. Thread needle with some white quilting thread and knot the end.

4. Fold the first loop so that the knot is at the top. Your needle will go through the two thicknesses of ribbon at the bottom.

Diagram 1

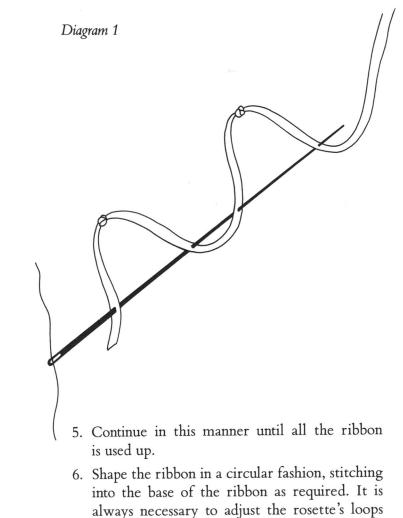

5. Continue in this manner until all the ribbon is used up.

6. Shape the ribbon in a circular fashion, stitching into the base of the ribbon as required. It is always necessary to adjust the rosette's loops until the desired effect is obtained.

7. Once the rosette is to your liking, stitch in position on the bib to cover the ends of the wider ribbon.

8. Repeat for other rosette.

EMBROIDERED HAT BAND

Embroidered hat bands make delightful gifts and are quick and easy to complete. Scraps of piping and fabric can be used up on small projects such as this, so don't be in a hurry to throw leftovers out.

DESIGN 1

MATERIALS

One straw hat

For brim of hat, 1.5 m (1⅔ yd) Liberty bias binding 4.5 cm (2″) wide, with both sides pressed under 7 mm (⁵⁄₁₆″) (either purchase it or make it yourself by cutting strips at 45° to the selvedge in the desired width)

For gathered trim on band, 1.2 m (1⅓ yd) strip of Liberty print fabric 5 cm (2″) wide

75 cm (28″) grosgrain ribbon 2.5 cm (1″) wide

1.2 m (1½ yd) mini double piping (narrow piping made up of two separate pieces of piping, in different colours, sewn together, available at specialist sewing shops)

Size 3 straw needle

DMC stranded threads:
Centre 893 Medium bright pink, Petals 894 Light bright pink, Leaves 958 Medium green

INSTRUCTIONS

1. Mark the centre of grosgrain ribbon by folding it in half. This denotes the position of the first embroidered motif.

2. Following the diagram, trace the design onto ribbon. It may be necessary to adjust the spacing of the roses or add extra ones, depending on the size of the crown of your hat.

Diagram 1

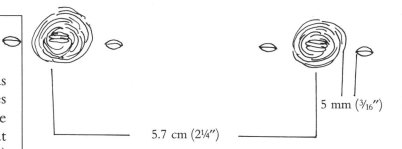

5 mm (³⁄₁₆″)

5.7 cm (2¼″)

The rose consists of three centre bullions in the darkest shade. Use a size 3 straw needle with six strands of thread. In order to produce a very full, raised centre, use 12 twists for these bullions.

The second and final round is in DMC 894, also using six strands but with 14 twists per bullion.

Leaves are two bullion stitches about 5 mm (a little more than ³⁄₁₆″) long using six strands of floss.

3. After embroidery is complete, wash the ribbon and block it flat to dry it.

4. Tack or baste the bias binding to the rim of the hat. Sew to hat using sewing machine and a regular straight stitch. (I used a size 70 jeans machine needle and matching thread.)

5. Try hat band around hat and mark the position where the two ends need to be stitched together.

6. With right sides together, stitch ends of hat band together and trim seam to 5 mm ($\frac{3}{16}$"). Press.

7. To apply double piping to edge of hat band, remove about 1 cm ($\frac{1}{2}$") of piping cord from one end of the piping. Fold this 1 cm ($\frac{1}{2}$") under.

8. Pin around the hat band, overlapping the piping at the join. In order to make this join as flat as possible, again remove about 1 cm ($\frac{1}{2}$") of cord from the piping to coincide with the overlap. Tack the double piping in position. Repeat for the other side.

9. With right sides together, join the Liberty print strip by the 5 cm (2") edges so that it forms a circle. Press this seam open and trim to 0.5 cm ($\frac{1}{4}$").

10. Fold circle in half along its circumference; press.

11. Run two rows of gathering 5 mm (a little less than $\frac{1}{4}$") and 7 mm (a little more than $\frac{1}{4}$") from the raw edge of this piece. Pull up gathers to fit hat band.

12. Pin gathered trim to hat band using the 5 mm gathering line to match the position where the tacking joins the piping and ribbon. Sew with a straight machine stitch, catching the piping and the gathered trim.

13. Remove all tacking threads; press. Fit hat band to crown of hat and sew into position.

DESIGN 2

MATERIALS

One straw hat

For brim of hat, 1.5 m (1$\frac{2}{3}$ yd) Liberty bias binding 4.5 cm (2") wide, with both sides pressed under 7 mm ($\frac{5}{16}$") (either purchase it or make it yourself)

75 cm (28") white grosgrain ribbon 4 cm (1$\frac{1}{2}$") wide

1.2 m (1$\frac{1}{3}$ yd) mini double piping in colours to match Liberty print fabric

75 cm (28") x 2.5 cm (1") wide Liberty print fabric that has had its edges pressed under 5 mm ($\frac{1}{4}$")

20 cm (8") x 115 cm (45") wide navy fabric

Madeira floss in 1007 Navy blue

Size 4 straw needle

INSTRUCTIONS

1. Centre the strip of Liberty fabric lengthwise on the grosgrain ribbon. Sew in position.

2. Fold the pair in half and mark. This denotes the position for the first embroidered motif.

3. Using a size 4 straw needle and four strands of Madeira 1007, work three bullion stitches using 10 wraps per bullion, as shown in diagram 2.

4. Continue embroidering as shown in diagram until sufficient ribbon is covered to go all the way around the crown of the hat.

Diagram 2

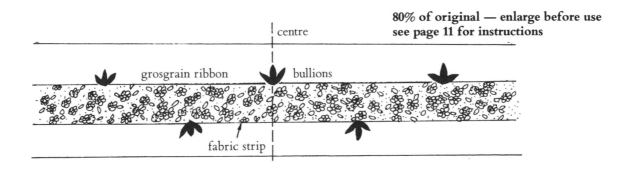

80% of original — enlarge before use see page 11 for instructions

centre

grosgrain ribbon   bullions

fabric strip

5. Try hat band around hat and mark the position where the two ends need to be stitched together.

6. With right sides together, stitch ends of hat band together and trim seam to 5 mm (³⁄₁₆″). Press.

7. To apply double piping to edge of hat band, remove about 1 cm (½″) of piping cord from one end of the piping. Fold this 1 cm (½″) under.

8. Pin around the hat band, overlapping the piping at the join. In order to make this join as flat as possible, again remove about 1 cm (½″) of cord from the piping to coincide with the overlap.

9. Tack the double piping in position. Repeat for the other side. Press well.

10. Stitch double piping in position on both edges. Remove tacking and press well.

11. Tack or baste the bias binding to rim of hat. Sew to hat using sewing machine and a regular straight stitch. (I used a size 70 jeans needle.)

12. For the bow, cut a piece of fabric 20 x 100 cm (8″ x 39″). Fold in half lengthwise, with right sides together; press.

13. The edges of the tie are angled. To do this, make seams as shown in diagram 3. Stitch, remembering to leave an opening to turn sash through.

14. Turn sash through to right side, press well. Slip stitch opening closed. Tie sash in a bow and handsew to hat to cover seams in hat band.

Diagram 3

DESIGN 3

MATERIALS

One straw hat

For brim of hat, 1.5 m (1²⁄₃ yd) Liberty bias binding 4.5 cm (2″) wide with both sides pressed under 7 mm (⁵⁄₁₆″) (either purchase it or make it yourself)

0.75 m (28″) white grosgrain ribbon 2.5 cm (1″) wide

For bow, 20 cm (8″) x 90 cm (36″) Liberty print fabric

For frills on side of band, 20 cm (8″) x 90 cm (36″) wide Liberty print fabric

Size 9 crewel needle

Size 7 straw needle

DMC floss: 3350 Dark pink, 894 Light pink, 958 Green, 798 Blue, 340 Mauve and 743 Yellow

INSTRUCTIONS

1. Measure the amount of grosgrain ribbon required to go around crown of hat. Mark approximate seam position with fabric marker.

2. Transfer design onto ribbon using a washout fabric marker. It may be necessary to adjust embroidery design in order to cover the entire length of ribbon. It is easy to do this by altering the spacing slightly between the floral motifs.

3. Embroider design as in the diagram.

   All embroidery, with the exception of the French knots, is worked using a size 9 crewel needle. The French knots are completed with a size 7 straw needle. Lazy daisies, stem and French knots are the only stitches used.

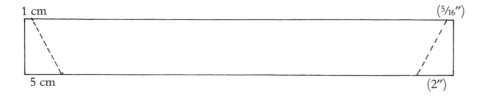

1 cm   (⁵⁄₁₆″)

5 cm   (2″)

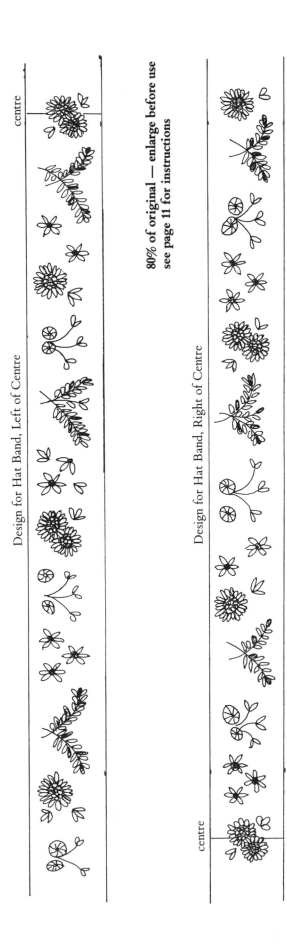

Design for Hat Band, Left of Centre

centre

80% of original — enlarge before use
see page 11 for instructions

Design for Hat Band, Right of Centre

centre

DMC 3350 — two strands for French knots in centre of pink daisy.

DMC 894 — two strands for lazy daisy stitch for petals on pink daisy.

DMC 958 — one strand for stems and lazy daisy leaves.

DMC 798 — two strands for lazy daisy stitch for blue flowers.

DMC 340 — two strands for lazy daisy stitch for mauve flowers.

DMC 743 — two strands for lazy daisy stitch for yellow flower. Three strands for French knots at centre of mauve flowers.

4. Once the embroidery is complete, wash the ribbon and block it flat to dry it.

5. Tack or baste the bias binding to the rim of the hat. Sew to hat using sewing machine and a regular straight stitch. (I used a size 70 jeans machine needle and matching thread.)

6. Try hat band around hat and mark the position where the two ends need to be stitched together.

7. With right sides together stitch ends of hat band together and trim seam to 5 mm (³⁄₁₆″). Press.

8. Cut four strips of Liberty fabric 90 cm x 5 cm (36″ x 2″). Join two of these strips to form a circle. Repeat for the other two strips. Press seams open.

9. For both circles, and with wrong sides together, fold fabric in half lengthwise. Press well.

10. Run a gathering thread 1 cm (³⁄₈″) from the raw edge on each piece. Run another gathering thread between the first line of stitching and the raw edge on both fabric circles.

11. Gather the two pieces of fabric to fit the embroidered hat band. Pin in position, adjusting gathers as necessary. Sew through all layers. Press. Handsew hat band in position on hat.

12. To make fabric bow, cut a piece of fabric 90 cm x 20 cm (36″ x 8″). Fold in half, with right sides together, and press.

13. Seam as shown in diagram. Remember to leave an opening along the straight edge to turn through.

Diagram 5

½ cm   (³/₁₅″)

2.5 cm   (1″)

14. Turn through to right side and press. Slip stitch opening closed. Tie in a bow and hand stitch in position at back of hat to cover join in hat band.

page 114

A pretty jewellery roll embroidered inside and out

Detachable collar featuring lavender and roses

Page 88

page 106

Matching lingerie and pot pourri sachets

Finely embroidered ring bearer's pillow

Baby's day gown with the special touch of buttons sewn on using bullion stitch pg 104

OAT-HANGER COVERS

MATERIALS

Per hanger cover, 15 cm x 115 cm (6″ x 45″) silk dupion

Per hanger cover, 1 m (40″) entredeux

Madeira silk floss: 506 Dark pink, 504 Medium pink, 502 Light pink (Design 2 only), 1510 Green

Size 9 straw needle

Size 9 crewel needle

3 m (3⅓ yd) lace 8 cm (3″) wide for Design 1

3 m (3⅓ yd) lace 6 cm (2¼″) wide for Design 2

3 m (3⅓ yd) lace 5 cm (2″) wide for Design 3

30 cm (12″) ribbon 1.5 mm (¹⁄₁₆″) wide for Designs 1 and 3

50 cm (20″) ribbon 1.5 mm (¹⁄₁₆″) wide for Design 2

6 tiny pink glass beads for Design 1

Per hanger, 30 cm x 50 cm (12″ x 20″) wadding

Wooden coat-hanger with brass hook (we had regular coat-hangers electroplated at minimal cost)

Thread to match fabric

INSTRUCTIONS

1. Trace all patterns onto lightweight interfacing including the embroidery design.

2. Cut a piece of fabric for front of hanger 15 cm (6″) long x 55 cm (22″) wide. Mark the centre.

3. Zigzag around the edges of fabric to prevent fraying.

4. Centre the pattern piece on fabric and trace the embroidery design onto the fabric in the appropriate location.

5. Embroider designs.

DESIGN 1

All bullions are worked with a size 9 straw needle. All stem stitch is embroidered with a size 9 crewel needle. Embroidery uses one strand of Madeira silk floss.

Five inner petals in Madeira 506 are each made from one bullion stitch with 10 wraps per bullion.

The outer petals (two per dark pink bullion) in Madeira 504 consist of 12-wrap bullions.

All leaves are 8-wrap bullions. Stems are in stem stitch in Madeira 1510.

DESIGN 2

The rose centres are in Madeira 506. They consist of three 8-wrap bullions.

The first round is in Madeira 504 with 10 wraps per bullion.

The second round is in Madeira 502 with 12 wraps per bullion.

The leaves are 8-wrap bullions in Madeira 1510.

The stems are in stem stitch in Madeira 1510.

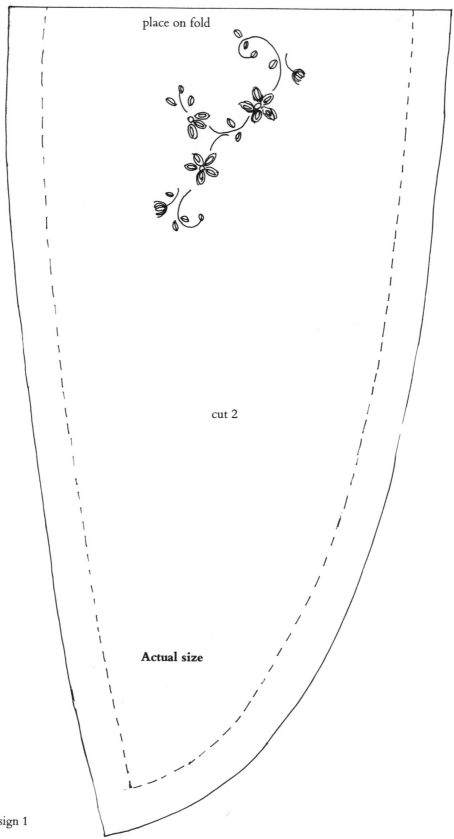

place on fold

cut 2

Actual size

Coat-hangers — Design 1

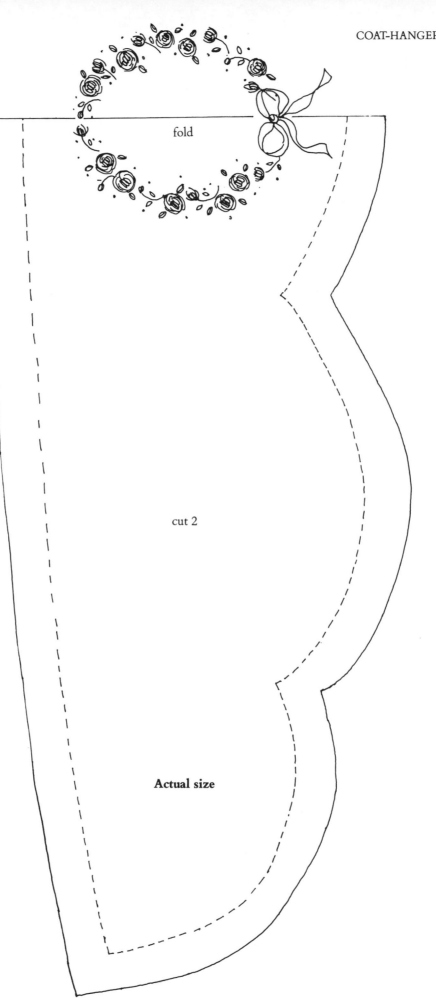

fold

cut 2

Actual size

Coat-hangers — Design 2

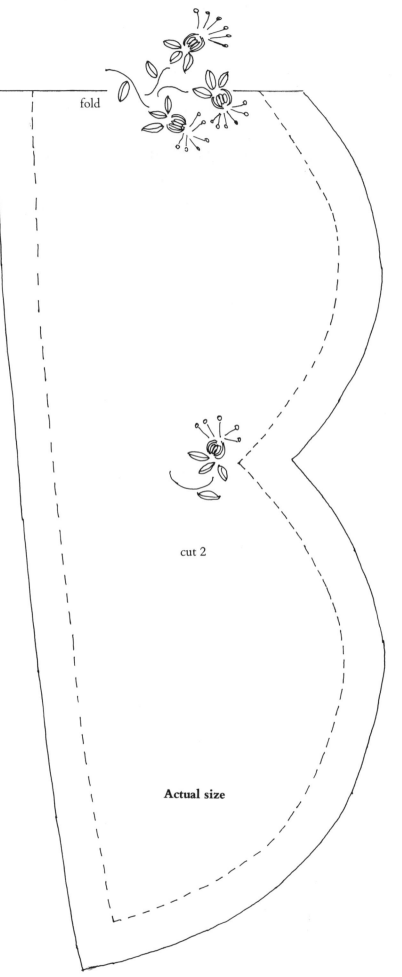

fold

cut 2

Actual size

Coat-hangers — Design 3

DESIGN 3

The outer elongated petals consist of double cast-on stitch in Madeira 506. There are 16 cast-ons per petal.

The inner petals are comprised of bullion stitch in two colours. The innermost three bullions are in Madeira 506 and have 10 twists per bullion. The two outer bullions, which encase these three, are in Madeira 504, and consist of 14 wraps each.

The stamens are in pistal stitch in Madeira 504.

The leaves are three bullion stitches in Madeira 1510. The central bullion has 12 twists and the two that encase it have 14 twists.

6. Rinse fabric to remove all traces of fabric marker. Press well.

7. Cut out the front of hanger ensuring that embroidery design is in the correct position.

8. From remaining fabric, cut out back of hanger.

9. Using a 1 cm seam (a little less than ½″) and leaving the opening indicated on the pattern piece, stitch back and front together.

10. Open seam out and press. There is no need to neaten this seam because it will be totally enclosed when the coat-hanger cover is finished.

11. Trim one side of the entredeux and clip into the batiste strip on the other side.

12. With right side of entredeux to right side of fabric, shape the entredeux around the bottom of hanger cover. Pin in place.

13. Stitch in the ditch of the entredeux.

14. Trim seam allowance to 5 mm (³⁄₁₆″) and press to the wrong side.

15. Whip gathered lace to the entredeux, either by hand or using a zigzag stitch on the sewing machine.

16. Fold wadding in half and cut a tiny hole in the top to allow the coat-hanger hook to go through.

17. Fit wadding over hanger and tack in position close to the wood of the hanger.

18. Using the pattern for the appropriate cover, trim the wadding to match the shape of the cover. Remember to take off the 1 cm (a little less than ½″) seam allowance.

19. Fit the cover over the hanger and pin bottom edges together.

20. Hanger cover can be completed by either machine stitching along the outside edge through all thicknesses or hand whipping the edges together under the trim.

21. Tie a ribbon on hook and secure it with a few small handsewn stitches.

FACE WASHER AND HAND TOWEL

It's great to embroider towels and ready-made linen; after the embroidery is complete, there's no drudgery of construction. Towels and face washers make excellent presents and can be tailored to suit any decor.

For this project I have used a hand-dyed thread. Never be afraid to try different threads to give your work a new, fresh look. The addition of beads to embroidery adds to the overall impact.

MATERIALS

One skein of Grevillea Kaleidocolours or
  similar variegated thread
Size 18 tapestry needle
Beading needle
Blue washout marker
One light-green face washer
One light-green hand towel
Assorted small beads to tone with towels and
  embroidery thread
Thread to match towels

INSTRUCTIONS

1. Draw the design onto the face washer and towel.

2. Follow the diagrams given to embroider the towel and face washers.

3. When embroidery is complete, add the beads using thread to match the towel.

4. Rinse in cold water to remove marking pen.

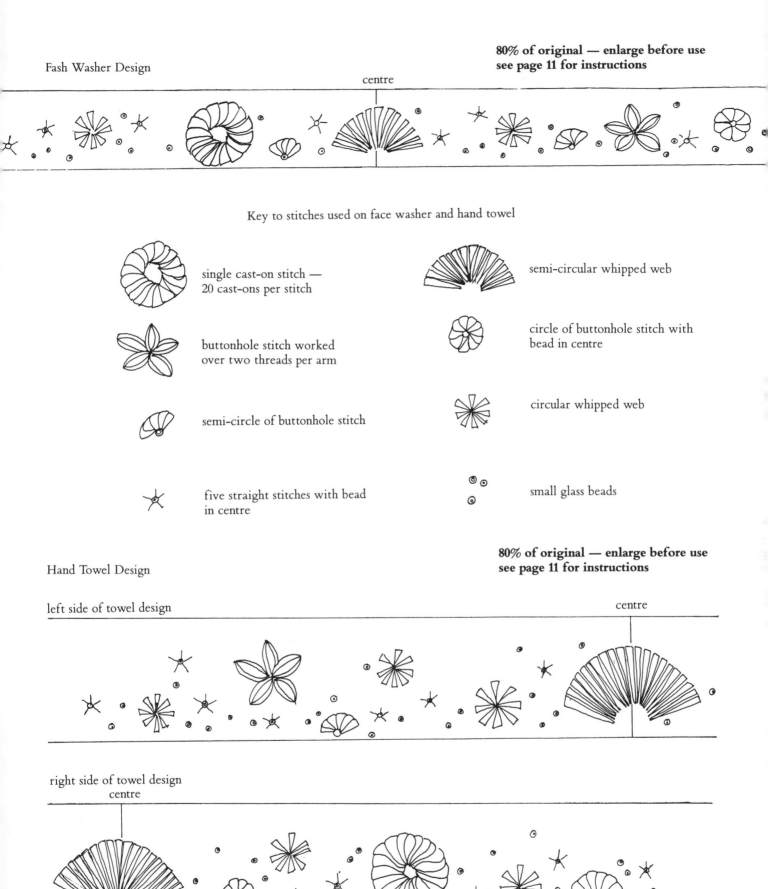

Fash Washer Design

80% of original — enlarge before use see page 11 for instructions

centre

Key to stitches used on face washer and hand towel

single cast-on stitch —
20 cast-ons per stitch

semi-circular whipped web

buttonhole stitch worked
over two threads per arm

circle of buttonhole stitch with
bead in centre

semi-circle of buttonhole stitch

circular whipped web

five straight stitches with bead
in centre

small glass beads

80% of original — enlarge before use see page 11 for instructions

Hand Towel Design

left side of towel design

centre

right side of towel design
centre

DETACHABLE COLLARS

By making a collar detachable, you extend the life of both the garment and the collar itself. It is possible to make any collar detachable by using any one of the three methods featured here.

1. A complete collar that 'sits' over the main garment. The collar is not attached to the main garment in any way. It can be worn with a number of garments providing the necklines match or the neckline of the collar itself lies above that of the garment.

2. Detachable collar with attachable facing. A facing is incorporated in the collar and press studs are attached to the inside neckline of the garment and the collar facing. This type of collar is usually limited to use on one main garment. It allows the usefulness of a main garment to be extended. For example, a plain white cotton collar for daytime could be exchanged for a satin collar for evening use.

3. False front. The collar is attached to a small amount of material so it can be worn under a jumper to give the appearance of a blouse.

Whichever style of detachable collar you use depends on the effect that you want to achieve.

COMPLETELY DETACHABLE COLLAR

Embroidered collars are best lined so that the full impact of the embroidery is seen. I usually make the neckline of the collar 5 mm (¼″) higher than that of the garment so that none of the garment appears above it. Simply add 5 mm (¼″) to the

neckline seam allowance and then use the normal pattern seam allowance. I do not usually interface detachable collars because this adds to the bulk and can cause them to 'poke' rather than sit down flat.

Detachable collars can have any decorative trim you like; a particularly pretty one is entredeux and whipped lace. Sometimes students feel intimidated by sandwiching entredeux between two layers of fabric, especially if there are sharp points. However, this is not difficult if you follow the method below.

1. Cut one embroidered collar and one plain collar.

2. Set the plain collar aside. You will be using a number of strips of entredeux depending on how many right-angled or sharp curves there are. Wherever entredeux must go around a right angle, or near right angle, it is important to overlap the entredeux.

Diagram 1

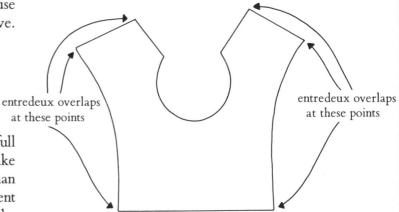

entredeux overlaps at these points

entredeux overlaps at these points

3. Cut the required number and lengths of entredeux strips.

4. Trim one side of the batiste strip from the entredeux on each piece.

5. On the embroidered collar, place the entredeux around the edge so that the batiste strip is level with the collar and entredeux overlaps at the sharp point. Pin in place.

Diagram 2

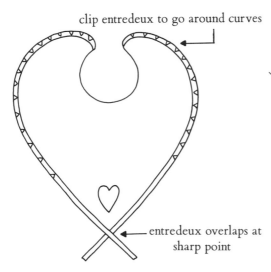

clip entredeux to go around curves

entredeux overlaps at sharp point

6. At the point where the two strips of entredeux overlap, trim the other side of the batiste strip — but only as much as the overlap.

Diagram 3

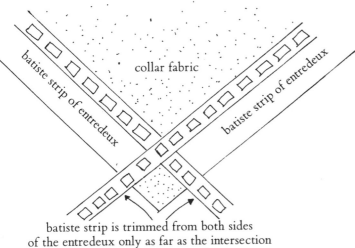

collar fabric

batiste strip of entredeux

batiste strip of entredeux

batiste strip is trimmed from both sides of the entredeux only as far as the intersection of the two strips of entredeux

7. Very carefully stitch in the ditch of the entredeux right around the collar. At the points where the entredeux overlaps, fold it back so it is not caught in the stitching. The pivot of the machine stitch will be in the collar fabric alone.

Diagram 4

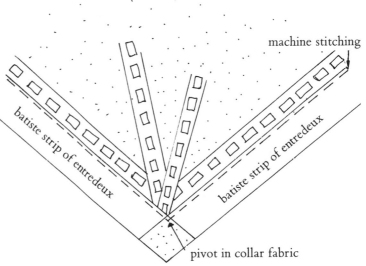

machine stitching

batiste strip of entredeux

batiste strip of entredeux

pivot in collar fabric

8. With the tails of the overlapping entredeux pinned away from the stitching line, and right sides together, pin the collar lining to the collar.

9. Using the previous stitching line as a guide, stitch the embroidered collar to the lining. If the neck edge is being finished at this time, remember to leave an unstitched area so that the collar can be turned through.

10. If there is likely to be a ridge of fabric when the collar is turned through, you must graduate the seam allowances. The neck curves, and any other curves, need to be clipped at this point.

11. Turn collar through to the right side and press.

12. At the point where the entredeux overlaps, trim both pieces to form a neat point. The two pieces of unattached entredeux will be sewn together when the lace is whipped on.

13. Slip stitch the opening closed.

14. You are now ready to whip lace to the entredeux.

DETACHABLE COLLAR WITH ATTACHABLE FACING

This type of detachable collar is used where the collar is worn solely with a particular garment. It is ideal when the laundering requirements of the main garment differ from that of the collar; for example, a wool crepe dress with a linen collar.

1. A facing needs to be cut to fit the garment on which the collar is going to be used. To do this, pin front and back pattern pieces together at the shoulder.

2. Measure 7.5 cm (3″), including neck seam allowance, from pattern edge.

Diagram 5

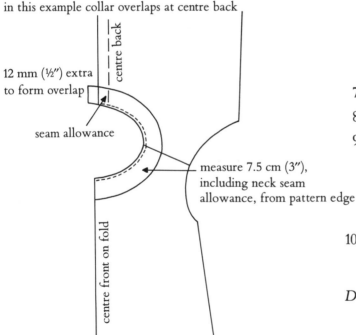

in this example collar overlaps at centre back

12 mm (½″) extra to form overlap

centre back

seam allowance

measure 7.5 cm (3″), including neck seam allowance, from pattern edge

centre front on fold

In this example collar overlaps at centre back.

3. Trace off this pattern, being sure to mark the centre back and front.

4. In the position where the collar will overlap, either centre back or front, add 12 mm (½″) plus the seam allowance on each side. A press stud will be sewn to this overlap to ensure the collar sits correctly.

5. Once the pattern for the facing has been drafted, cut two of these facings in fabric. The construction of the collar can begin.

6. With right sides of the collar together, stitch around the outside edge. Leave neck edge unfinished.

Diagram 6

7. Trim and clip seams as required.

8. Turn to right side and press.

9. With right sides together, place a facing piece on each side of the collar so that the collar is sandwiched between the two facings. Be sure to match centre fronts of the collar and facing.

10. Stitch in place around the neck edge and across the ends of facings.

Diagram 7

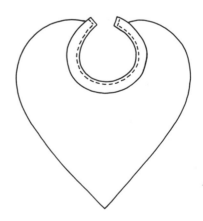

11. Clip neck and trim seam to 3 mm (⅛″).

12. Turn facing through to right side and press well.

13. In order to make the facing sit down correctly, stitch 2 mm (1/16″) from the edge of facing through all thicknesses.

Diagram 8

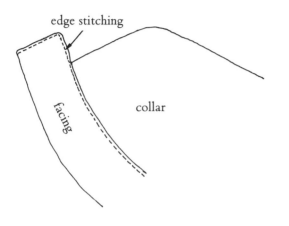

edge stitching

facing

collar

14. Press well.

15. Finish raw edges of facing either by overlocking them together or by using a decorative edge stitch (such as scallops) on your sewing machine.

16. Place the collar around the neckline of the garment to check fit. Press studs are sewn to the underside of the collar facing and the inside of the garment to secure the collar. Usually three or four press studs are sufficient. Where the facing overlaps I like to add a press stud so that the edges of the collar 'sit' in the desired position.

FALSE FRONTS

These are made on much the same lines as the faced detachable collars but the facing is a longer flap and the flap is not attached. The length of the flap secures the collar in position.

This type of attachable collar is usually used with sweaters or jumpers. To make a false front, draft a flap off your favourite blouse pattern.

1. Measure down about 20 cm (8″), or desired length, from shoulder seam on front and back. Remember to add a seam allowance to the centre front (for a front closing).

Diagram 9

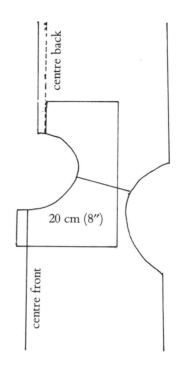

centre back

20 cm (8″)

centre front

2. You should have two pattern pieces that look like those shown in diagram.

Diagram 10

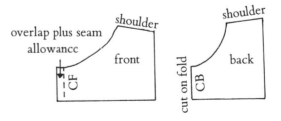

overlap plus seam allowance

shoulder

front

CF

shoulder

cut on fold

CB

back

3. Cut two backs on the fold and four fronts. Join one set of fronts to each back. Press seams and trim to 3 mm (⅛″).

4. Any type of collar can be added to a false front. Before cutting out the collar of your choice, it is essential to check that the neckline of the collar and the flap match. Make any adjustments required to the neck of the collar.

The chosen collar can now be made up completely, except for the neckline.

5. With right sides together, sandwich the neck of the collar between two sets of false fronts.

6. Stitch around neckline and entire outer perimeter of false front as shown in the diagram. Be sure to leave an opening to permit turning.

Diagram 11

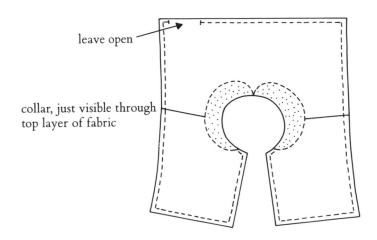

leave open

collar, just visible through top layer of fabric

7. Clip and trim all seams. Turn through to the right side and press well.

8. Slip stitch opening closed.

9. Sew press studs in the required positions down the front to secure.

Parasol Collar

This was made as a completely detachable collar to fit a child who is a size 5. It looks wonderful over an apricot coloured velveteen dress.

MATERIALS

50 cm (20″) ecru Swiss batiste. Mine was supplied by Capitol Imports
3 m (3⅓ yd) edging lace 3 cm (1¼″) wide, such as Capitol Imports lace 2025

DMC floss: 350 Very deep apricot, 351 Deep apricot, 352 Medium apricot, 353 Light apricot, 522 Green
1 m (40″) ecru entredeux
Size 10 straw needle
Size 9 straw needle
Size 10 crewel needle
A blue Dixon marker or similar
Thread to match fabric

INSTRUCTIONS

1. Trace design onto the fabric using the Dixon marker.

2. Using the crewel needle, work the parasol first in a single strand of DMC 352.

3. Now work the daisies. They have centres of French knots made from two strands of 351; use the size 9 straw needle. The petals are in 353 and consist of 10-wrap bullions worked with the size 10 straw needle.

4. The five-petal flowers are worked following the instructions for bullion forget-me-nots (see pages 45-6). The double bullion petals are in DMC 352, and have eight twists per bullion; they are worked with the size 10 straw needle. The centres are French knots in two strands of DMC 350; use a size 9 straw needle.

5. All leaves consist of two bullions in DMC 522 and are of approximately eight twists per bullion.

6. The stems are worked in outline stitch using one strand of 522 and the crewel needle.

7. Buds are two bullion stitches in DMC 352, with eight wraps per stitch. They are surrounded by two fly stitches in 522.

8. The baby's breath is made of French knots in two strands of 353. It is worked with the size 9 straw needle.

9. Complete all embroidery and then rinse the fabric to ensure all the lines made by the marker are removed. Allow to dry. Iron the wrong side, with the right side placed face

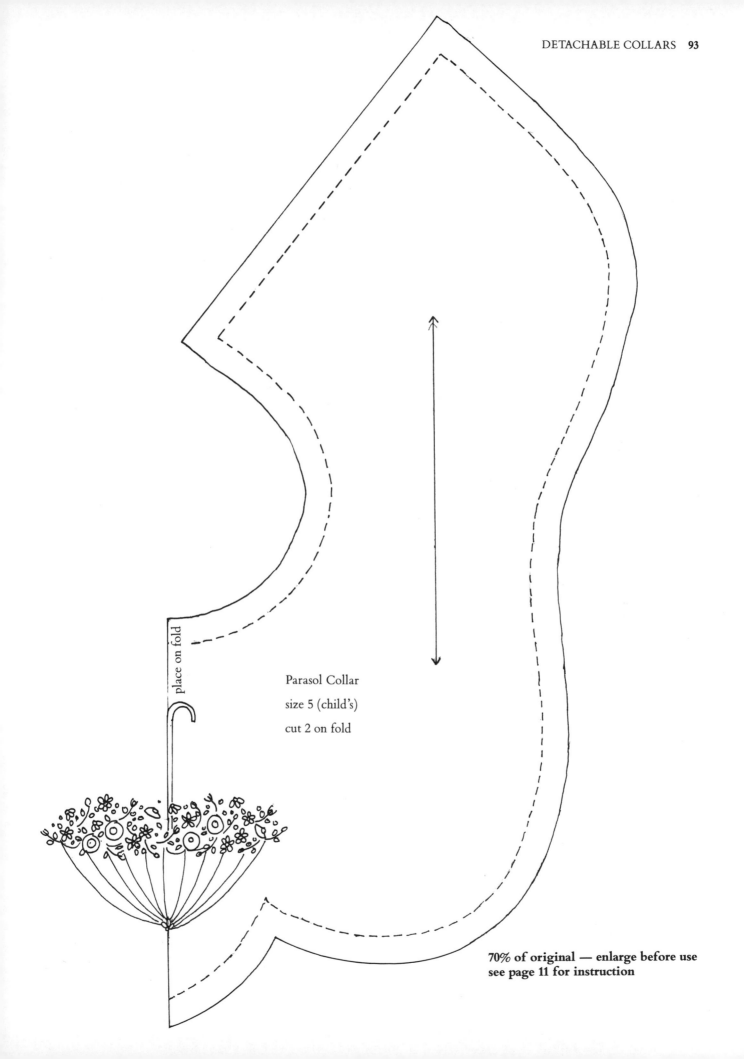

place on fold

Parasol Collar

size 5 (child's)

cut 2 on fold

**70% of original — enlarge before use
see page 11 for instruction**

down in a towel to avoid flattening the embroidery.

10. Cut the collar out and make up following the instructions for a detachable collar.

11. Hand whip lace to collar.

12. Attach a button and loop to close collar.

Embroidery Design for Parasol Collar

80% of original — enlarge before use see page 11 for instructions

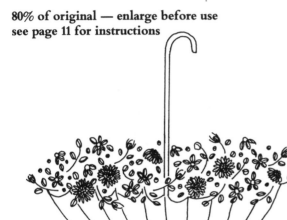

ROSE AND LAVENDER COLLAR

This design is worked on white cotton voile in Madeira silk floss. It is the type of design that would be suitable for either an older child or an adult's garment. The silk floss washes well so there are no problems with laundering.

MATERIALS

Size 9 straw needle for bullions

Size 9 crewel needle for shadow work and stem stitch

Madeira silk floss: 504 Deep rose, 503 Medium rose, 502 Light pink, 803 Lavender, 1510 Green

50 cm x 115 cm (20″ x 45″) white voile

3 m (3⅓ yd) lace 5 cm (2″) wide. I used Capitol Imports lace No. 2026

1 m (40″) white entredeux

Thread to match fabric

INSTRUCTIONS

1. Using a Dixon marker or similar, draw the design onto a rectangle of fabric of sufficient size to cut out the collar.

2. Complete the shadow work bow and ribbon first, using one strand of Madeira 803.

3. Now work the bullion roses.

4. The roses consist of three central bullions in Madeira 504. Each bullion has eight wraps.

5. The next row is in 503, with 10 wraps per stitch.

6. The final row is in 502, with 12 wraps per bullion.

7. The buds are two 8-wrap bullions in 504, surrounded by two fly stitches in 1510.

8. All leaves are made up of two bullion stitches in 1510, with each bullion consisting of eight wraps.

9. The stems are also worked in 1510, but are done in outline stitch with the size 9 crewel needle.

10. For the lavender, work the green (1510) stem first. The bullions are worked from the top of the stem down.

11. The bullion at the top of the stalk has 10 wraps. As you proceed down the stem, gradually increase the number of wraps to a maximum of 14 at the bottom of the stem.

12. Once all embroidery is complete, rinse the fabric to remove all traces of the marker. Allow to dry. Press by placing the embroidery face down on a soft, thick towel and ironing the wrong side.

13. Cut out the collars from the embroidered and plain fabrics. Assemble as per the instructions in Detachable Collars (see pages 88-9).

14. Hand whip lace to the collar. Add a button and make a loop for the back of the collar.

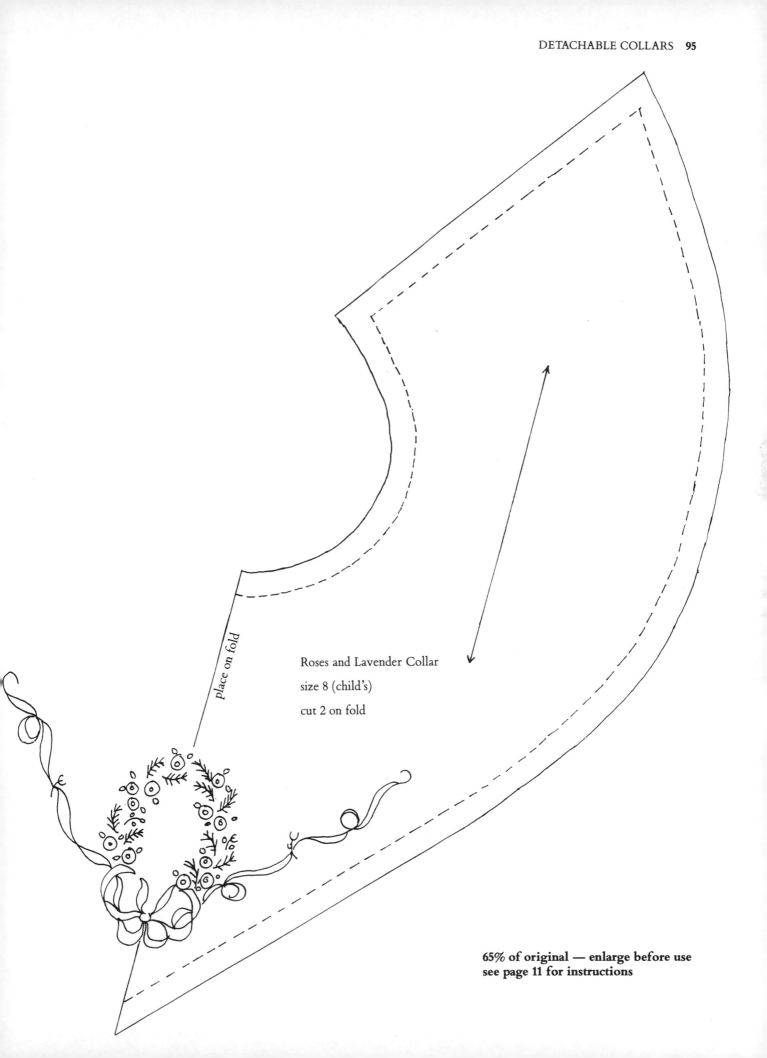

place on fold

Roses and Lavender Collar

size 8 (child's)

cut 2 on fold

**65% of original — enlarge before use
see page 11 for instructions**

Design for Roses and Lavendar Collar

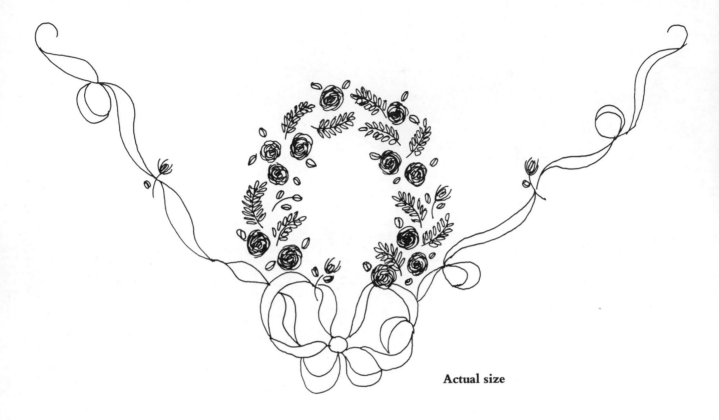

Actual size

An elegant selection of coat hangers

page 81

Three embroidered hankies make a special gift

Chatelaine with dainty sprays of embroidered flowers

page 130

Satin robe with delicately embroidered collar

page 141

A collection of cushions featuring patchwork, ribbon work and bullion embroidery

Holly buttons give a Christmas look to a purchased shirt

page 134

Embroidered hand towels and face washer to brighten up the bathroom

BABY DAY GOWN

MATERIALS

1.50 m (1⅔ yd) x 115 cm (45″) wide white Swiss voile

5.40 m (6 yd) white lace edging 2.5 cm (1″) wide. You will need 1.5 m (1⅔ yd) for left side of front band; 2.5 m (98″) for right side of front band and neck; and 1.4 m (1½ yd) for sleeves

1.60 m (64″) entredeux

40 cm (16″) entredeux beading

50 cm (20″) wide blue ribbon 7 mm (about ¼″) wide to match embroidery thread

60 cm (24″) white cotton bias binding to finish sleeve seam allowance (optional)

Small amount of DMC stranded thread in 3755 Light blue and 368 Light green

Seven 10 mm (⅖″) buttons with four holes in each

Size 10 straw needle

Size 10 crewel needle

INSTRUCTIONS

1. Cut two pieces of fabric as per diagram below.

2. Pull threads on fabric as indicated on the diagram. Only pull the thread 10 cm (4″) *not* the length of the fabric. Leave the excess thread hanging on the wrong side of the fabric. These lengths will be darned in when the tucks are finished off.

3. Tucks are made by folding along pulled thread line and stitching 3 mm (⅛″) from the fold. This can be accomplished easily on Bernina

Diagram 1

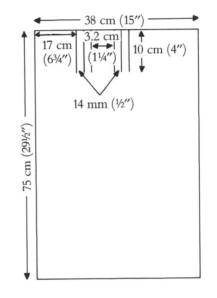

1130 or 1230 machines by placing the fold under the presser foot at the centre mark and de-centring the needle to the maximum left position. Those using other machines should consult their manuals to see if it is possible to de-centre the needle and how it is done.

4. Tucks need to be finished off by taking the threads to the wrong side. Tie the threads off and then darn some of the excess into the wrong side of the tuck to secure it. Darn in the pulled threads to secure.

5. Press completed tucks towards armhole curve.

6. Using the appropriate pattern piece and a washout marker, trace the embroidery design onto the two tucked pieces of fabric.

7. Embroider design.

8. Rinse fabric to remove tracing line. Allow to dry and then press well.

9. Using the appropriate pattern pieces, cut out left and right fronts, ensuring tucks and embroidery are in their correct position. Also, cut out front band and front facing.

10. With right sides together, place a strip of entredeux down the facing side of the right front.

11. Place the front band on top with its raw edges level with the edge of the right front. The entredeux is now sandwiched between the front band and the right front.

12. Stitch in the ditch of the entredeux, which should be just visible through the front band.

13. Press and trim the seam to 3 mm (⅛″).

14. Place a strip of entredeux down the other side of the front band and then place the front facing on the top, with its right side down. Once again the entredeux is between two layers of fabric.

15. Stitch in the ditch of the entredeux.

16. Trim seam to 3 mm (⅛″) and press well.

17. Fold the first half of the facing in and press.

18. Fold facing in so that the first folded edge is level with the wrong side of the front band. Press well.

19. Slip stitch front facing to the wrong side of front band.

20. Work seven button holes in the front band in the position indicated on the pattern (7 cm/ 2¾″) apart.

21. Trim the batiste strip from the entredeux that is attached to the front band.

22. Whip gathered lace down the entredeux on the left side of the front band as shown below. Do not add any lace to the other side of the band at this stage. See diagram 2.

23. Fold in left front facing on first fold line. Press.

24. Fold facing on second fold line. Press and then slip stitch in position.

Diagram 2

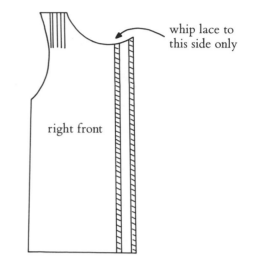

whip lace to this side only

right front

25. To form kick pleat in back of day gown, fold from the line marked on the pattern to the centre back on each side.

26. Top stitch pleat 3 mm (⅛″) from the folded edge on each side. Remember only to stitch the depth indicated on the pattern. Press well.

27. Join fronts to back using a French seam at each shoulder. Press.

28. Mark a 1 cm (½″) seam allowance around the neck. Stitch on this line, using a small, straight machine stitch.

29. Press machine stitching flat. Trim fabric to within 2 mm (¹⁄₁₆″) of machine stitching line.

30. Roll and whip neck edge using a zigzag stitch on the sewing machine.

31. Cut a piece of entredeux sufficient to go around neckband; have 2 cm (1″) extending beyond the front bands.

32. Trim the batiste strip from one side of the entredeux and clip the other at 1 cm (½″) intervals.

33. Attach the entredeux to the neck edge using a zigzag stitch on the sewing machine. Press. (For details on this see construction chapter pages 54–5.)

34. Trim batiste strip from neck edge. Bend the overhang of the entredeux level with the right and left fronts.

35. Take 2.5 m (2½ yd) edging lace (this allows for a fullness of 3:1) and gather it by pulling a thread in the lace heading. Neatly finish one end of the lace by turning under twice and handstitching in place. With right sides together, and starting at the left front, whip gathered lace around the neck edge and down the front band to the hem line. Finish lace at hem line using this same method. Press.

36. Finish side seams with French seams.

37. Cut two pieces of entredeux beading 18 cm (7″) long for armbands.

38. French seam under arm of both sleeves. Press seam towards back.

39. Roll, whip and gather the lower edge of the sleeve.

40. Join entredeux beading to form a circle, using a 5 mm (¼″) seam allowance. Finish the seam allowance with a close zigzag.

41. Trim batiste strip from both sides of the entredeux beading.

42. Gather 70 cm (28″) edging lace. Attach to one side of the entredeux beading band. Repeat for other band.

43. Run a row of gathering 1 cm (½″) from the armhole edge and between the notches.

44. Thread ribbon through the entredeux beading and handstitch to secure.

45. Gather sleeves to fit armholes. Adjust gathers and stitch in position.

46. Trim sleeve seam to 5 mm (¼″) and then either neaten with a close zigzag, or bind edges with bias binding.

47. Ensure bottom edge of dress is even. Trim if necessary. Turn under 5 mm (¼″) and press.

48. Machine stitch along this 5 mm (¼″) seam allowance with a small, straight machine stitch. There will be some puckering of the fabric.

This is intentional as it removes the excess fullness and negates the need to have small pleats in the finished hem.

49. Fold up hem 5 cm (2″) or desired amount. Slip stitch in position.

50. Work bullions and lazy daisies to attach buttons. The bullions require 20 twists per stitch.

EMBROIDERY DESIGN FOR BETWEEN THE TUCKS

All embroidery is worked in one strand of floss. A size 10 straw needle is used for bullions and a size 10 crewel for back stitch.

Leaves are two bullion stitches with six wraps per stitch in DMC 368.

Flowers are three 8-wrap bullion stitches in DMC 3755.

The stems are back stitched in DMC 368.

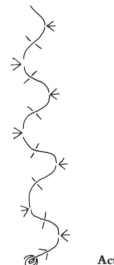

Actual size

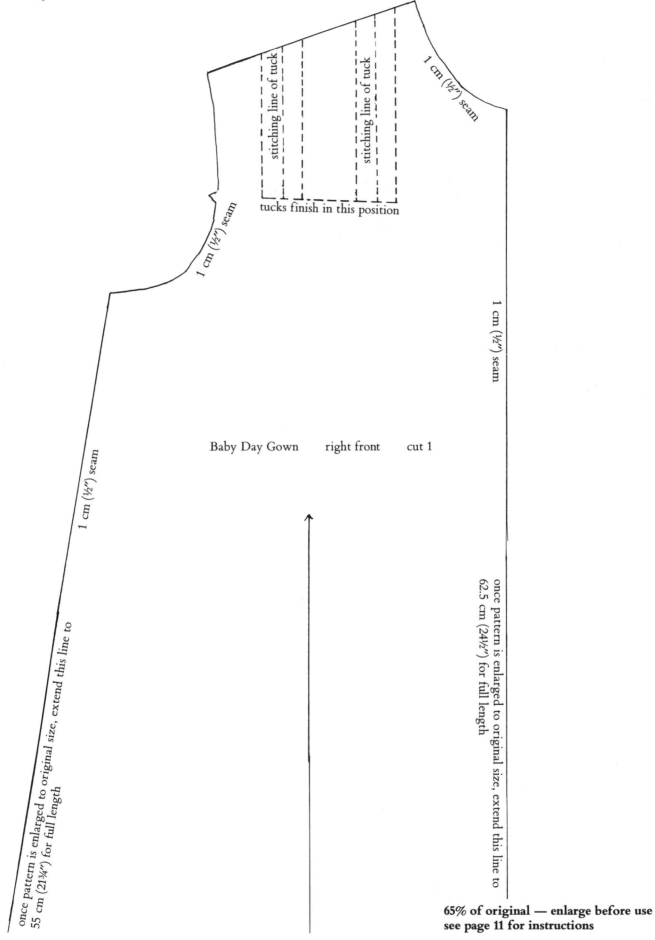

stitching line of tuck

stitching line of tuck

1 cm (½″) seam

tucks finish in this position

1 cm (½″) seam

1 cm (½″) seam

1 cm (½″) seam

Baby Day Gown right front cut 1

once pattern is enlarged to original size, extend this line to 55 cm (21¾″) for full length

once pattern is enlarged to original size, extend this line to 62.5 cm (24½″) for full length

65% of original — enlarge before use see page 11 for instructions

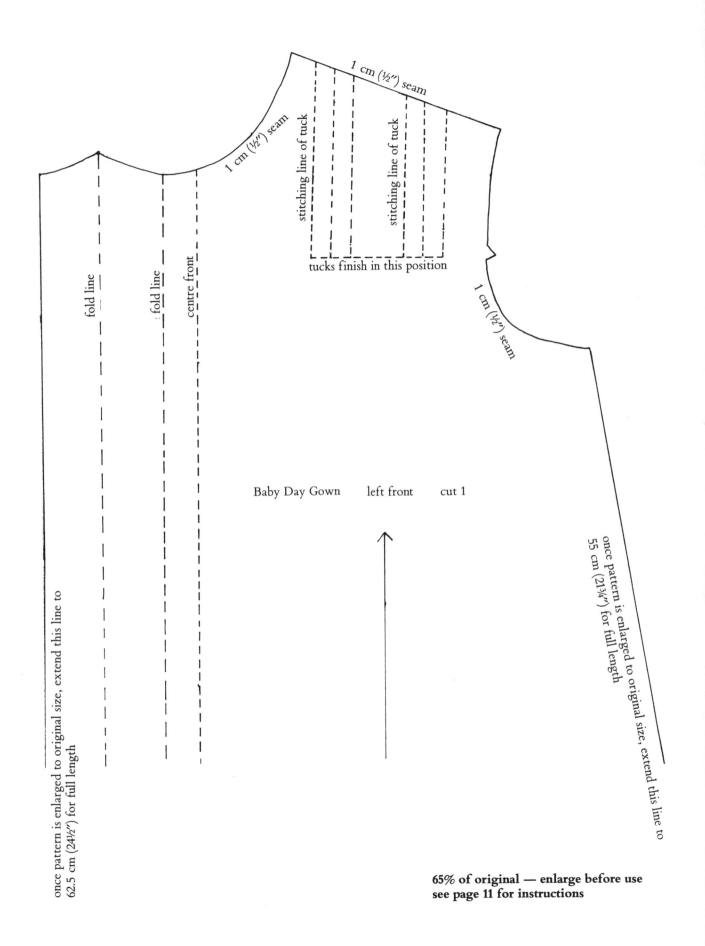

1 cm (½") seam

1 cm (½") seam

stitching line of tuck

stitching line of tuck

tucks finish in this position

fold line

fold line

centre front

1 cm (½") seam

Baby Day Gown   left front   cut 1

once pattern is enlarged to original size, extend this line to 62.5 cm (24½") for full length

once pattern is enlarged to original size, extend this line to 55 cm (21¾") for full length

**65% of original — enlarge before use
see page 11 for instructions**

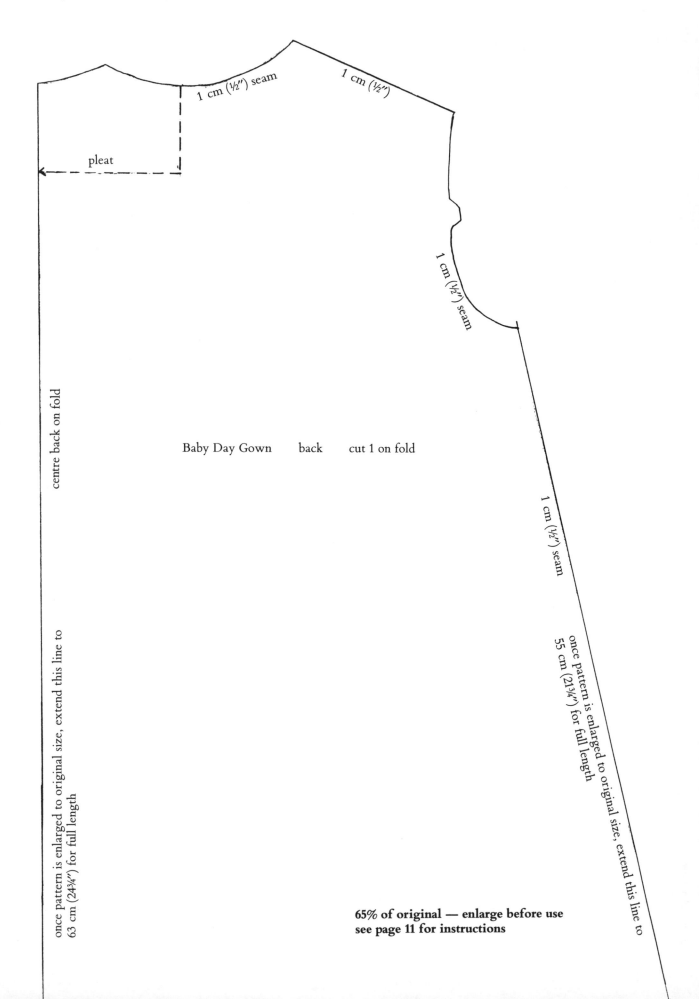

pleat

1 cm (½″) seam

1 cm (½″)

1 cm (½″) seam

centre back on fold

Baby Day Gown   back   cut 1 on fold

once pattern is enlarged to original size, extend this line to 63 cm (24¾″) for full length

1 cm (½″) seam

once pattern is enlarged to original size, extend this line to 55 cm (21¾″) for full length

**65% of original — enlarge before use
see page 11 for instructions**

once pattern is enlarged to original size, extend this line to
63 cm (24¾″) for full length

1 cm (½″) seam

attach to right front band

fold line

Baby Day Gown   right front facing   cut 1

once pattern is enlarged to original size, extend this line to
63 cm (24¾″) for full length

**65% of original — enlarge before use
see page 11 for instructions**

1 cm (½″) seam

attach to right front

centre front

attach to right front facing

1 cm (½″) seam

1 cm (½″) seam

Baby Day Gown   right front band   cut 1

once pattern is enlarged to original size, extend this line to
64 cm (25″) for full length

once pattern is enlarged to original size, extend this line to
62.5 cm (24½″) for full length

1 cm (½″) seam

½ cm (¼″) seam

Baby Day Gown   sleeve   cut 2

**65% of original — enlarge before use
see page 11 for instructions**

1 cm (½″) seam

SINGLET AND PANTIES

A dilemma I often have is wanting to embroider something for a new arrival but just not having the time. To overcome this, I simply 'personalise' a purchased baby garment. Singlets and pants are a good idea as a new Mum can never have too many of these.

MATERIALS

One baby singlet in an appropriate size
One pair of baby pants
Size 9 straw needle
DMC floss: 341 Blue (776 or 223 if you prefer pink), 523 Green
50 cm (20″) ribbon 2 mm (¹⁄₁₆″) wide to match embroidery floss
Small bodkin to thread ribbon
Blue washout marker

INSTRUCTIONS

The embroidery is best done on the solid bands, as opposed to the knitted fabric, of the singlet. It is possible to embroider the knitted fabric, but it is much more difficult.

1. Draw embroidery design on singlet and panties.

2. Using the straw needle, and two strands of the blue floss, make three 12-twist bullions; finish off.

3. Using the size 9 straw needle and two strands of green floss, make two 10-twist bullions on each side of the flower.

4. Repeat for remaining design.

5. Repeat for flowers on panties.

6. Rinse in cold water to remove marker.

7. Thread ribbon around neck using bodkin. Tie in a bow. Trim ends as required.

Embroidery Design
for Baby's Singlet

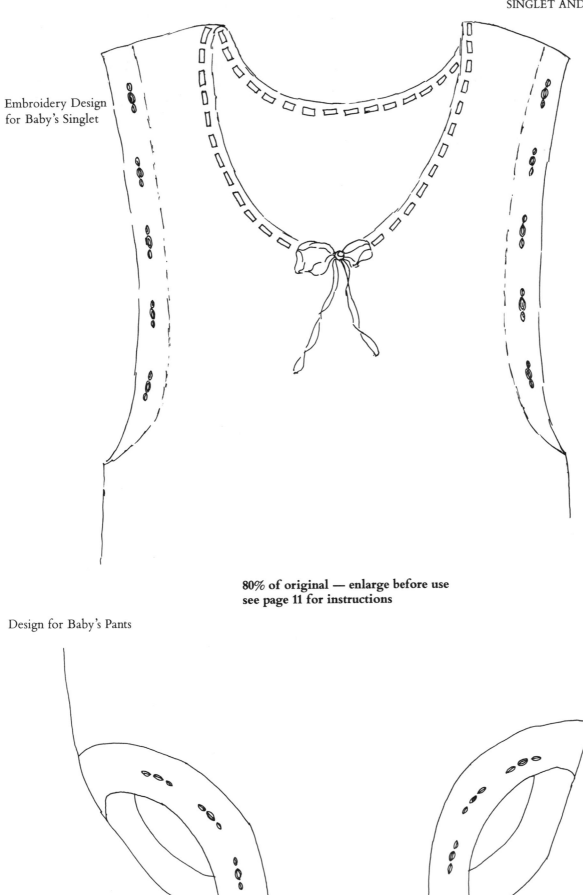

**80% of original — enlarge before use
see page 11 for instructions**

Design for Baby's Pants

 LINGERIE AND POT POURRI SACHETS

MATERIALS

75 cm (30") x 115 cm (45") ivory Swiss batiste

1.6 m (1⅔ yd) champagne entredeux

3.5 m (3⅘ yd) champagne lace edging 3 cm (1¼") wide. (I used Capitol Imports No. 2315.)

25 cm (10") champagne lace edging 12 mm (½") wide. (I used Capitol Import No. 2314).

DMC floss: 224 Light rose, 223 Medium rose, 3721 Dark rose, 522 Green

A small amount of pot pourri

Size 10 straw needle

Size 10 crewel needle

Embroidery Design for Lingerie Sachet

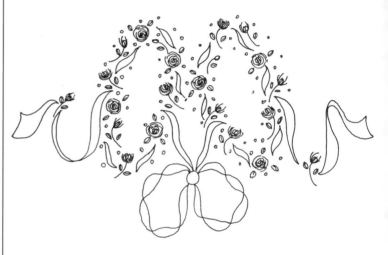

**80% of original — enlarge before use
see page 11 for instructions**

INSTRUCTIONS

1. Trace embroidery design onto a piece of fabric 50 cm x 40 cm (20" x 16") for the lingerie sachet, and 30 cm x 15 cm (12" x 6") for the pot pourri sachet. Ensure that the designs are centred and that there is sufficient fabric for cutting out pattern pieces once embroidery is complete.

2. Complete the shadow work on the ribbon in the design first, using one strand of 223.

3. Now work the bullion roses in one strand of embroidery floss. The centres consist of three bullion stitches, each of eight wraps of 3721. The first round is of five to six bullion stitches with 10 wraps of 223 per bullion. The second, and final round, consists of about seven to eight bullion stitches, or sufficient to encircle the

Embroidery Design for Pot Pourri Sachet

Actual size

first round, with 12 twists per bullion. Colour 224 is used for this round.

4. The 'side on roses' can now be done. Their centres are of two bullion stitches in 3721. Seven wraps per bullion are required. The first round consists of three to four bullion stitches with nine wraps; use 223. The second round is of five to six bullion stitches in 224, using 11 wraps per bullion.

5. The buds consist of two adjacent bullions with eight wraps per bullion; use one strand of 223. They are encased by two fly stitches in 522.

6. The leaves can now be worked in one strand of 522. There are two stitches with eight wraps per bullion.

7. Now work stems in outline stitch, using one strand of 522.

8. The baby's breath is now worked in French knots. Use two strands of 224.

9. Wash the embroidered pieces to remove all marks and allow to dry. Iron on wrong side, placing embroidery face down in a thick towel.

10. Position the pattern pieces on fabric, centring the embroidery design and transferring all markings. Cut out all pattern pieces.

FOR THE LINGERIE SACHET

1. Trim one side of the entredeux and press. Place untrimmed side of entredeux to the external edge of the sachet, and, with the right sides together, pin entredeux around the entire perimeter. Remember to clip curves where necessary.

Diagram 1

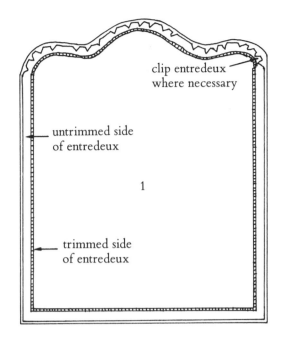

2. Stitch in the ditch of entredeux.

3. Pin pattern piece 1 to 2 with the right sides together.

Diagram 2

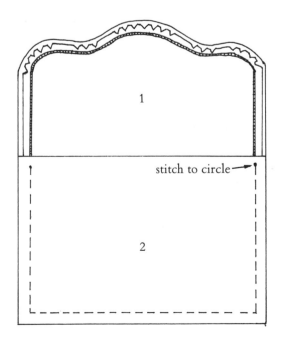

4. Stitch pattern piece 1 to 2 on outside perimeter using previous stitching, as shown in the last diagram, as a guide.

5. Trim all seams to 3 mm (⅛"). Turn sachet to right side and then press.

6. Fold pattern piece 3 on the fold line, with right sides together; press.

7. Stitch from fold to large dots.

Diagram 3

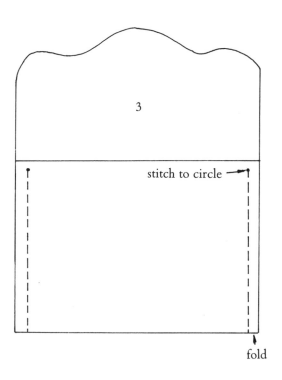

8. Trim seams to 3 mm (⅛"), and turn so the right sides are out. Press.

9. Put lining into sachet with right sides together. Pin around the curved top of sachet and across the opening. Ensure an opening is left on front flap for turning as shown in the diagram.

10. Stitch around sachet using previous stitching as a guide. Stitch through all thicknesses.

Diagram 4

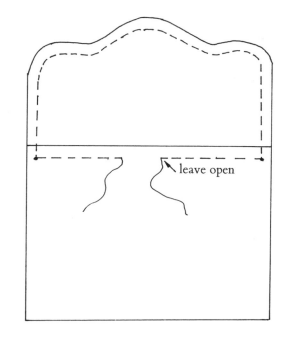

11. Clip curves around top of sachet and trim all seams to 3 mm (⅛").

12. Turn through unstitched portion so that right sides are out. Press. Sew a clear press stud to the underside of flap to close sachet.

13. Slip stitch the opening closed.

14. Gather lace by pulling a thread in the heading. Whip gathered lace to entredeux around the edge of sachet.

DIRECTIONS FOR POT POURRI SACHET

This consists of two pieces; a sachet and a pot pourri bag.

A. POT POURRI BAG

1. Cut a piece of fabric 20 cm x 10 cm (8″ x 4″).

2. Fold to form a 10 cm (4″) square with right sides together. Press.

3. Sew, using a 1 cm (½″) seam allowance around three edges. Remember to leave an opening on one side to permit turning.

4. Trim seams to 3 mm (⅛″).

5. Turn right sides out.

6. Fill with pot pourri and then slip stitch the opening closed.

B. SACHET

1. Cut out fabric, centring design as show on pattern.

2. Fold in half, wrong sides together. Press.

3. Machine down both sides using a 1 cm (½″) seam allowance. Trim seam to 3 mm (⅛″).

4. Turn inside out so that right sides are together. Sew down side seams again, making a 5 mm (¼″) seam allowance, to form a French seam. Press.

5. Apply lace to top of sachet with a small zigzag. Press.

6. Insert completed pot pourri bag and close the top by tying the ribbon. Finish ribbon in a bow.

Lingerie Sachet

pattern piece 2

cut 1

**60% of original — enlarge before use
see page 11 for instruction**

Lingerie Sachet

pattern piece 1

cut 1

**60% of original — enlarge before use
see page 11 for instruction**

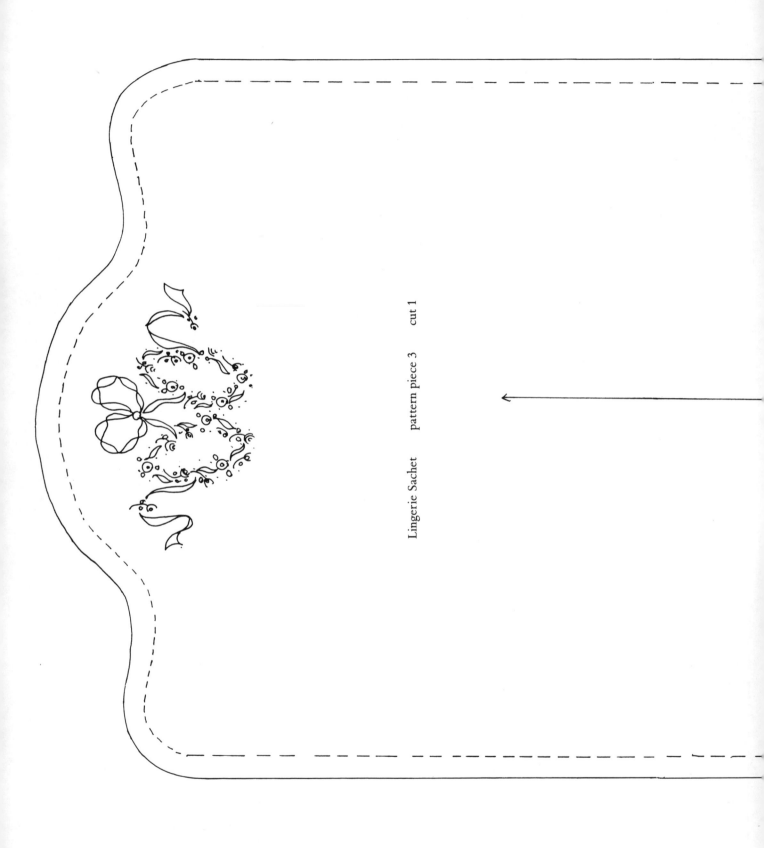

Lingerie Sachet   pattern piece 3   cut 1

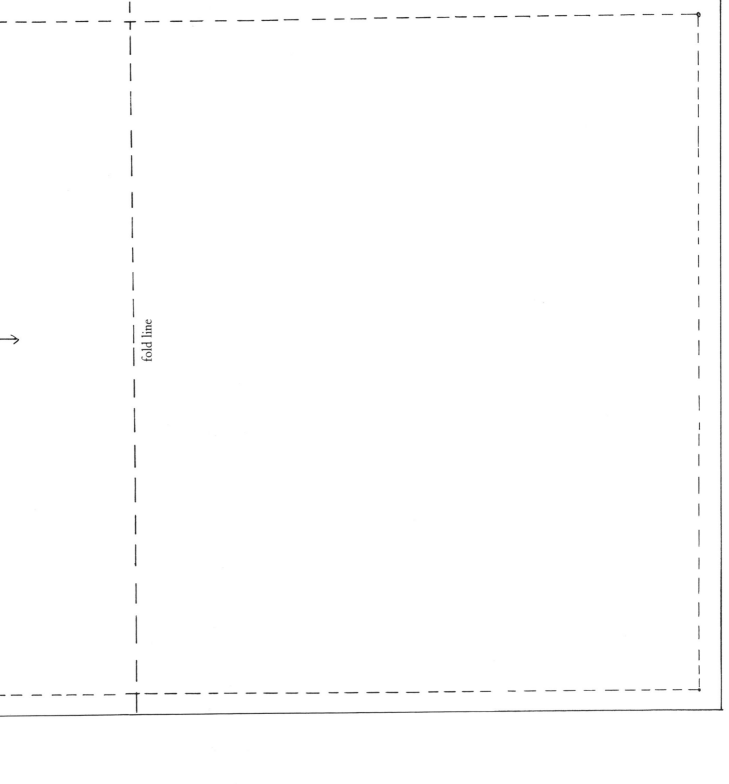

fold line

JEWELLERY ROLL

Silk is always special, so what better fabric than that for this luxurious jewellery roll? The embroidery is also in silk and is worked on both the outside and inside of the roll.

This extravagant jewellery roll would make a great gift for someone special. All the pockets are fully lined and it is finished with apricot satin piping.

The embroidery is relatively simple but the construction of this item does take time as all the pockets are lined and two zips have to be inserted. The finished product is well worth the effort.

MATERIALS

65 cm x 115 cm (26″ x 45″) cream silk dupion

Two 25 cm (10″) cream zippers

Lightweight interfacing onto which patterns can be traced

35 cm x 55 cm (14″ x 22″) piece of light-weight batting

One clear press stud or snap fastener

1.5 m (1½ yd) of apricot ribbon 3 mm wide, to match silk floss

1.5 m (1½ yd) of apricot satin mini-piping

Madeira silk floss: 0214 Dark apricot, 0303 Medium apricot, 0302 Light apricot, 1510 Medium green

Sizes 5 and 9 straw needles for bullions

Sizes 6 and 8 crewel or sharp needles for stem stitch

A fine needle suitable for handsewing and basting

Thread to match the cream silk

Dressmaker's carbon paper

INSTRUCTIONS

1. Trace the patterns and embroidery designs onto the interfacing. Be sure to include all the pattern markings to make assembling the jewellery roll easier.

   It is best to complete the embroidery before cutting out the pattern piece. The embroidery design is traced in the desired position onto a rectangle of silk a little larger than that of the pattern piece.

   For this project, I found that the designs were best applied to the fabric by using a carbon paper. I used yellow Clover Chacopy but any light coloured dressmaker's carbon would be suitable. Be sure to test a patch on your silk to see that your lines will be visible and that the carbon will wash out.

   Silk dupion has a strong tendency to fray, so zigzag around the edges of all these rectangles. This is why the rectangles of silk must be cut a little larger than the pattern pieces.

2. The embroidery is now ready to be worked. Madeira silk floss was used in my sample. This is similar to stranded floss except that each thread comprises four strands. Each strand is slightly thicker than one strand of DMC floss.

   The outside embroidery design is worked in four strands of floss using a size 5 straw needle for the bullions and a size 6 crewel needle for the stem stitch. The roses are made up of three bullions in the darkest shade of apricot, using eight twists per bullion. The bullions in the next round have 10 twists and are worked in 303. The final round is of 12-twist bullions in 302.

The inside embroidery is worked in one strand of floss using a size 9 straw needle for the bullions and a size 8 crewel needle for the stem stitch. Roses have eight twists per bullion in the centre, 10 twists per bullion in the next round and 12 twists in the final round. The colour arrangement is identical to that of the large roses. All leaves are bullions with seven twists.

Once embroidery is complete, wash all pieces in lukewarm water, using a mild detergent to remove all tracing lines. Rince thoroughly and wrap in a towel to remove excess moisture. Dry flat.

3. When dry, iron all pieces wrong side up. Use a clean towel between the ironing board and the silk to support the embroidery and prevent it being crushed.

Now cut all the pattern pieces required from the fabric. Because silk dupion frays very easily (as previously discussed) cut pattern pieces only as they are needed for assembly. The jewellery roll will be assembled in sections, so you can cut out pieces as you need them.

SECTION 1 — INSIDE POCKETS A & B, RING HOLDER AND FLAPS FOR POCKET C

4. Pattern pieces 1 (pocket A), 2 (pocket B) and 3 (ring holder) have an embroidered top section and a plain lining.

When cutting out embroidered pieces, it is essential that the embroidery is aligned with the correct position on the pattern piece.

Cut out two pockets A, and two pockets B, one from the appropriate embroidered rectangle and the other from plain fabric.

5. On both embroidered piece and lining, turn under a 1 cm (½″) seam allowance and press. This needs to be done on only one edge for pocket A, but on two edges for pocket B (see diagram 1 on page 117).

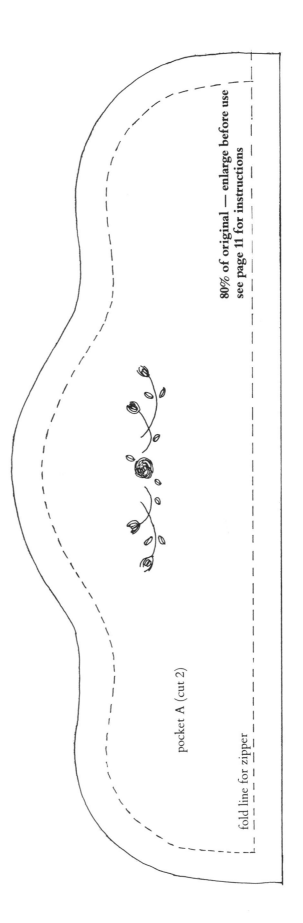

80% of original — enlarge before use
see page 11 for instructions

pocket A (cut 2)

fold line for zipper

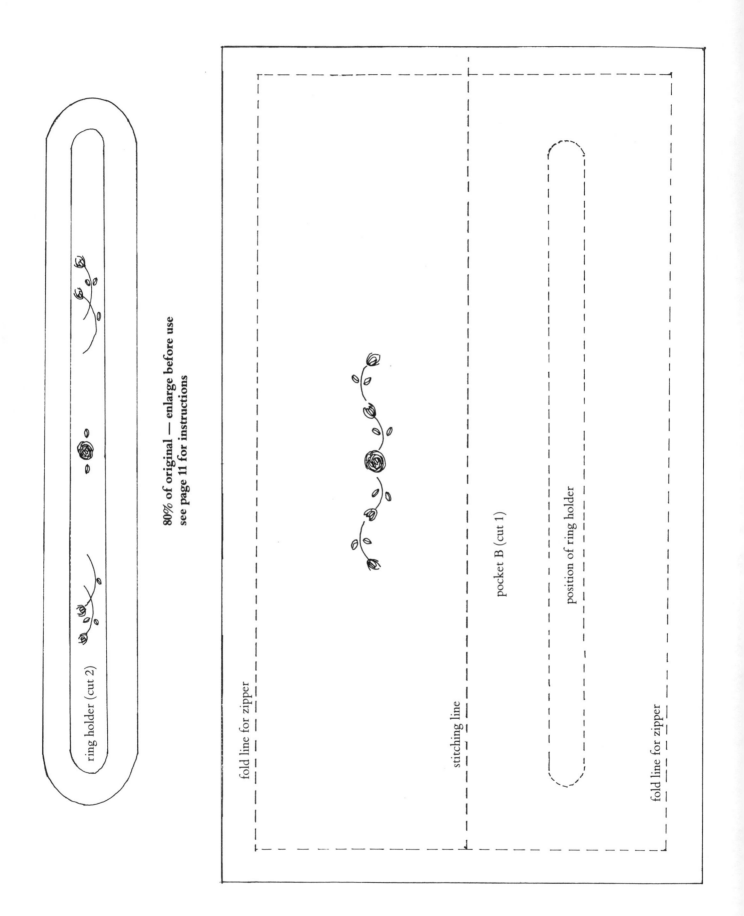

ring holder (cut 2)

80% of original — enlarge before use
see page 11 for instructions

fold line for zipper

stitching line

pocket B (cut 1)

position of ring holder

fold line for zipper

Diagram 1

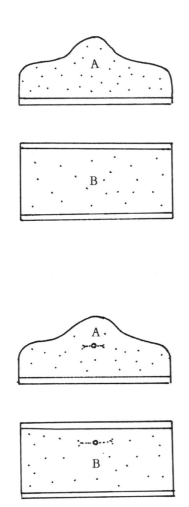

7. Take the embroidered piece for pocket A and its lining. With the zipper facing right side up, baste pocket A to the zipper and the lining fabric. The initial basting of the lining to the zipper may now be removed.

Diagram 3

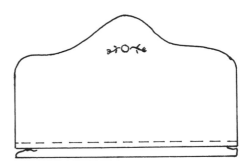

8. Stitch this side of zipper in position. Remove basting and press.

9. Take the lining fabric for pocket B. With wrong sides together, baste the lining fabric to the other side of the zipper (see diagram 4).

Diagram 4

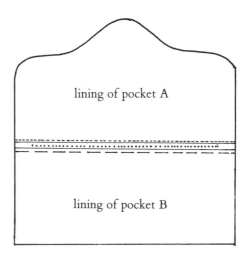

lining of pocket A

lining of pocket B

6. Take the lining of pocket A and baste the wrong side of the lining to the wrong side of the zipper, along the edge of the zipper as shown in diagram 2.

Diagram 2

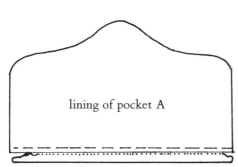

lining of pocket A

10. Using the embroidered piece for pocket B, and with the right side of zipper uppermost, baste pocket B along zipper edge (see diagram 5).

Diagram 5

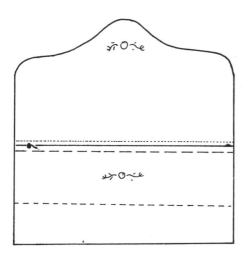

11. Remove original basting from lining.

12. Stitch zipper in place by going through all the thicknesses. Remove all basting and press.

13. Cut out two ring holders, one from the correct embroidered rectangle and the other from plain fabric. Cut eight flaps for pocket C.

14. With right sides together, sew around the ring holder; leave an opening to allow for turning.

15. Trim seams and turn through to the right side. Press and slip stitch the opening closed. Set aside.

16. With right sides together, sew around the three sides of each flap as shown in diagram 6.

Diagram 6

17. Trim seams and clip corners. Turn through to the right side and press (see diagram 7).

18. With wrong sides together, insert the four flaps across the bottom of pocket B. Baste in position.

Diagram 7

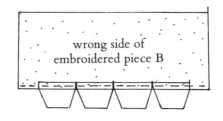

wrong side of embroidered piece B

19. Baste lining over the positioned pocket flaps through all thicknesses. The initial basting of flaps to embroidered piece can now be removed. Stitch the flaps to pocket B.

Diagram 8

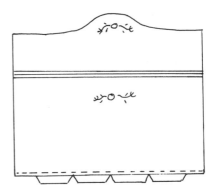

20. Sew the upper section of a press stud to the left underside of the ring holder. Sew the other side of the press stud to the correct position on pocket B.

21. Tie two tiny apricot bows in ribbon. Sew one in position above the press stud on the ring holder. Set the other bow aside.

22. Handsew the right-hand end of the ring holder in position on pocket B. Carefully sew the other apricot bow to cover this stitching. Fasten the ring holder.

This completes section 1.

SECTION 2: POCKETS C & D AND FLAPS FOR POCKET E

1. Cut one pocket C from correct embroidered rectangle. Cut one pocket D from appropriate embroidered rectangle and one from plain fabric. Cut four flaps for pocket E.

2. Fold under the 1 cm (½″) seam allowance on either side of pocket C and press as shown in diagram 9.

Diagram 9

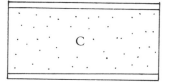

3. Fold pocket in half as indicated on pattern piece; press.

4. Baste the zipper between the two edges of pocket C (see diagram 10).

Diagram 10

5. Sew zipper in position on this edge.

Diagram 11

6. Press under the 1 cm (½″) seam allowance on both sides of pocket D for embroidered and plain piece.

7. With wrong sides together, baste the lining for pocket D to the zipper.

8. Now pin, and then baste, the right side of pocket D to the right side of the zipper. Remove first lot of basting; sew in place (see diagram 12).

Diagram 12

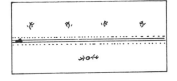

9. Remove all basting; press.

10. Take two flaps for pocket E, and, with right sides together, sew around the three sides.

Diagram 13

11. Trim seams and clip corners. Turn to right side and press. Repeat for other flap.

12. Carefully align the two flaps along the bottom of pocket D. They will lie against the embroidered fabric of pocket D. Baste in position. Now fold the lining down to cover where the flaps have been inserted. Baste. The initial basting can now be removed. Sew in position (see diagram 14).

Diagram 14

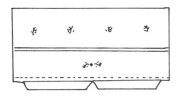

SECTION 3: POCKET E

1. Cut pocket E from embroidered rectangle. Fold in half and press. Set aside ready for next steps.

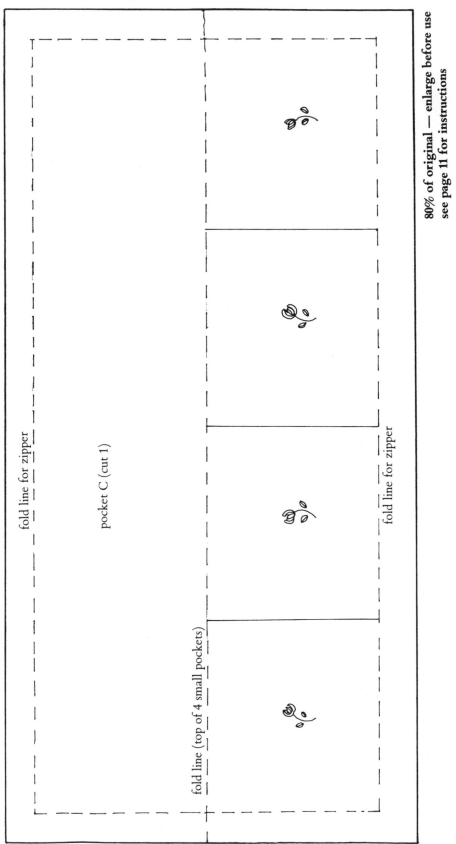

fold line for zipper

pocket C (cut 1)

fold line (top of 4 small pockets)

fold line for zipper

80% of original — enlarge before use
see page 11 for instructions

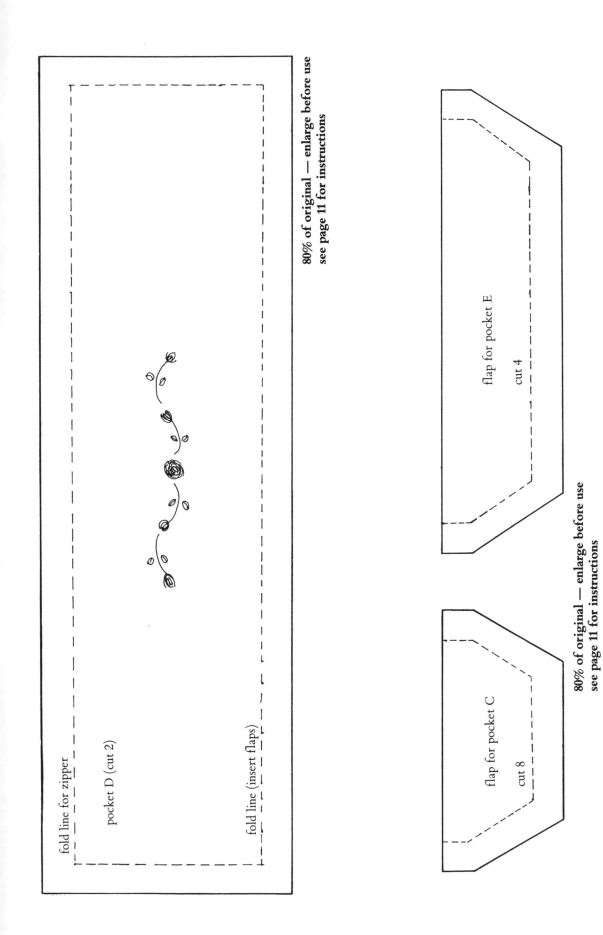

fold line for zipper

pocket D (cut 2)

fold line (insert flaps)

80% of original — enlarge before use
see page 11 for instructions

flap for pocket E

cut 4

flap for pocket C

cut 8

80% of original — enlarge before use
see page 11 for instructions

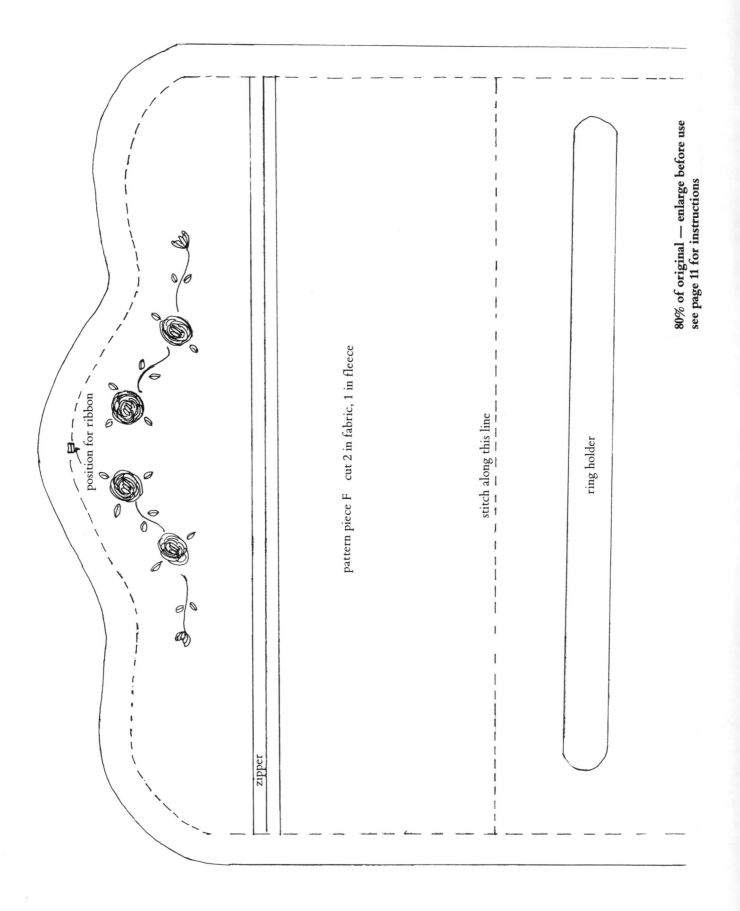

position for ribbon

zipper

pattern piece F   cut 2 in fabric, 1 in fleece

stitch along this line

ring holder

80% of original — enlarge before use
see page 11 for instructions

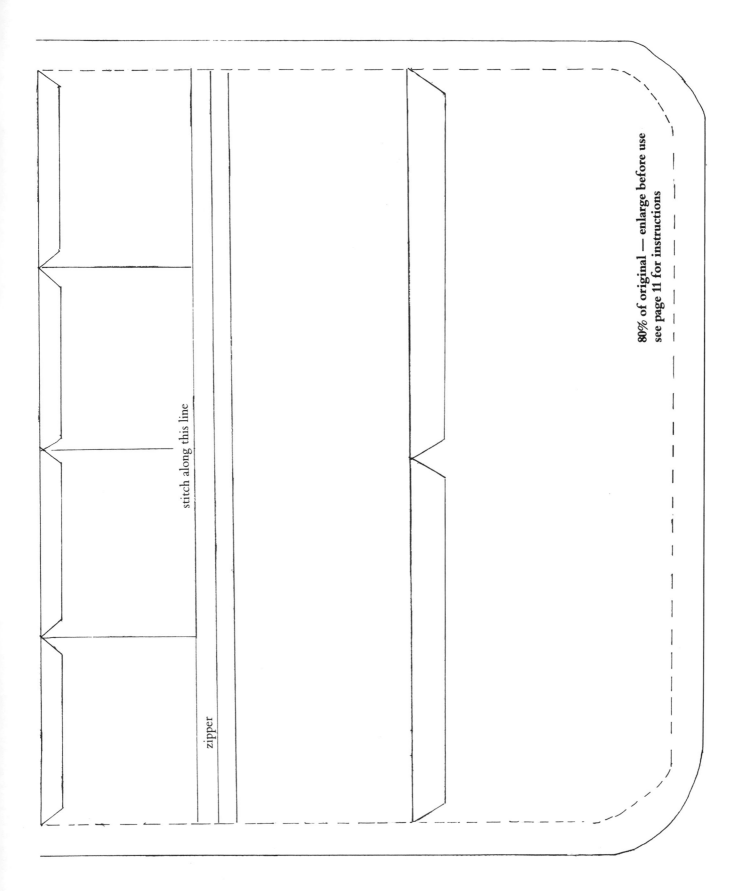

stitch along this line

zipper

80% of original — enlarge before use
see page 11 for instructions

pocket E (cut 1)

**80% of original — enlarge before use
see page 11 for instructions**

fold line for pockets (top of 2 large pockets)

SECTION 4

1. Take the lining section of piece F and lay it flat. Pin, then baste the previously prepared sections 1, 2, and 3 in position.

2. Stitch the pocket divisions on pieces C and E as indicated on pattern. Sew the lower limit of pocket B and also the lower limit of the four small pockets of C. Set aside.

3. From embroidered top piece, cut out pattern piece F, remembering to centre embroidery. Cut pattern piece F out in lightweight batting.

4. Baste the batting to the wrong side of the embroidered piece.

5. Fold ribbon in half and baste to the centre of the jewellery roll on the right side. (See diagram.)

6. On the right side, pin piping around the outside edge, clipping where necessary to go around curves, as shown in diagram 15.

7. Sew piping in position.

8. Trim batting very close to stitching line.

9. With right sides together, pin the two parts of the jewellery roll together.

10. Using the piping stitch line as a guide, stitch these two pieces together. Leave an opening at the bottom to allow for turning.

11. Trim all seams to 3 mm (⅛″) and clip curves. Turn through to right side.

12. Slip stitch opening closed. Press carefully. Roll up jewellery roll and tie ribbons to secure. Trim ribbons if required.

Diagram 15

RING CUSHION

Weddings are the most special of occasions; what better time to make a keepsake? Our ring-bearer's pillow is embroidered in bright spring colours but could easily be adapted to any bridal colour scheme.

MATERIALS

Madeira silk floss: 506 Dark pink, 504 Medium pink, 1107 Blue, 105 Yellow, 1114 Green, 902 Lavender
50 cm x 115 cm (20" x 45") cream silk dupion
1 m (40") ecru entredeux
3 m (3⅓ yd) edging lace 7.5 cm (3") wide. (I used Capitol Imports lace No. 6244 and dyed it ecru with coffee and vinegar)
Size 9 straw needle
Size 9 crewel needle
Thread to match fabric
25 cm (10") cream zipper (optional)
1 m (40") cream ribbon 1.5 mm (¹⁄₁₆") wide

INSTRUCTIONS

1. Enlarge design and trace onto a rectangle of fabric.
2. All bullions and French knots are worked with the straw needle. All other embroidery is worked with the crewel needle.
3. All embroidery uses single strand DMC floss.
4. The daisy petals use 504, and are made up of 10-wrap bullions, while the centres are French knots worked in 506.
5. The lavender features stem stitch in 1114. The bullions are in Madeira 902. Ten wraps are used at the top of the stem, increasing to 14 at the bottom.
6. The loop flower is made using 35 twists per bullion in 506; its centres are filled with French knots in 504.
7. The forget-me-nots had five petals in 1107 with two 8-wrap bullions per petal. The centre used French knots in 105.
8. The leaves, small mauve flowers and small yellow flowers are all worked in buttonhole stitch in the Madeira silk floss colours 1114, 902 and 105 respectively. These are spaced randomly throughout the design. The colour plate will act as a guide for the positioning of these motifs.
9. When embroidery is complete, wash fabric and dry it flat.
10. Iron on the wrong side, placing embroidery face down into a thick towel.
11. Cut out the embroidered front of cushion and a plain back from the pattern.
12. If required, a zipper can be inserted in the back of the cushion so that an insert can be used.
13. Insert entredeux around the outside of the cushion, following the instructions for adding entredeux to detachable collars (see page 88).
14. Sew back and front cushions together. Trim seam and neaten if required.
15. Turn through to right side.
16. Hand whip gathered lace to entredeux.

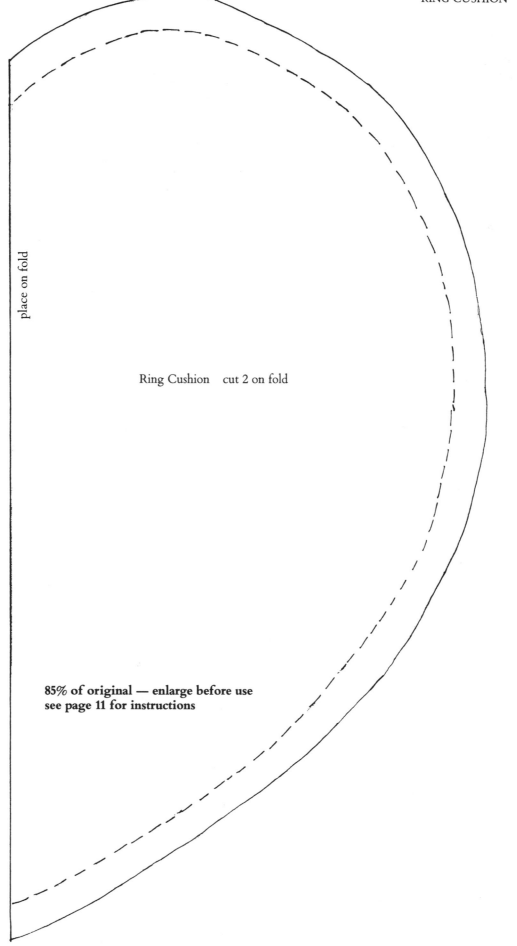

place on fold

Ring Cushion   cut 2 on fold

**85% of original — enlarge before use
see page 11 for instructions**

Embroidery Design for Ring Cushion

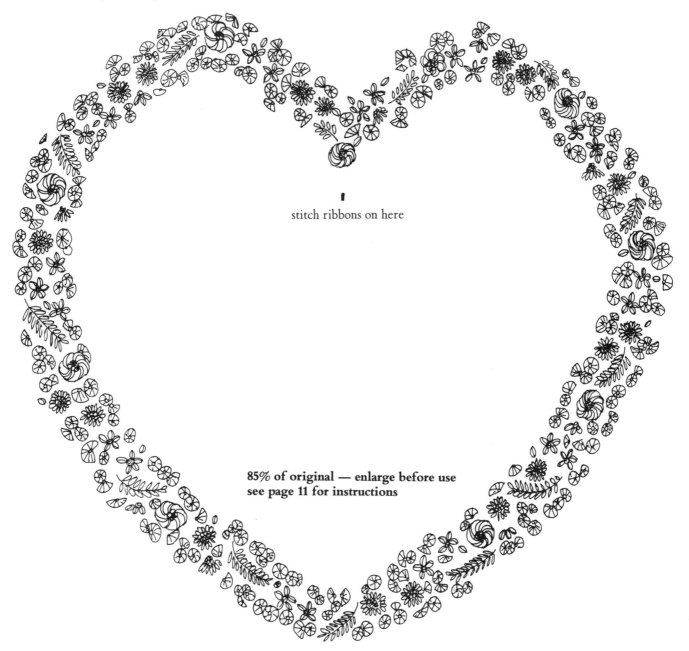

stitch ribbons on here

**85% of original — enlarge before use
see page 11 for instructions**

17. Cut the ribbon in half to make two 50 cm lengths. Mark the centres of each length. Place one on top of the other and hand stitch in the position indicated on the pattern.

18. Add insert or stuff the cushion with your chosen material.

19. To tie on the rings, place one ring on the left-hand side of piece A (see diagram 2) and the other ring on the right-hand side of ribbon B.

Diagram 1

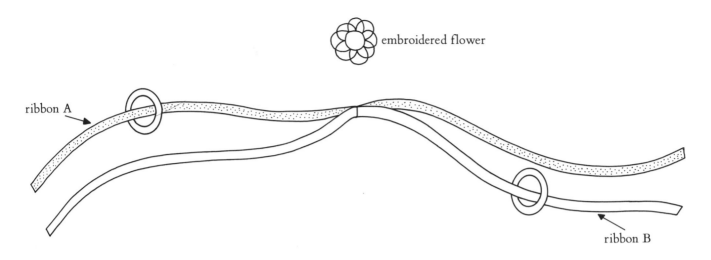

embroidered flower

ribbon A

ribbon B

20. Loop the ribbons to the desired length. Make sure that the tails of ribbon with the rings on them cross at the point where the ribbons are attached to the cushion. See diagram 2.

21. Tie the two extended pieces of ribbon together in order to hold the pieces with the rings on them firm.

22. Now put the two sections of ribbon A and B together and tie in a bow to secure. Trim excess ribbon from ends.

Diagram 2

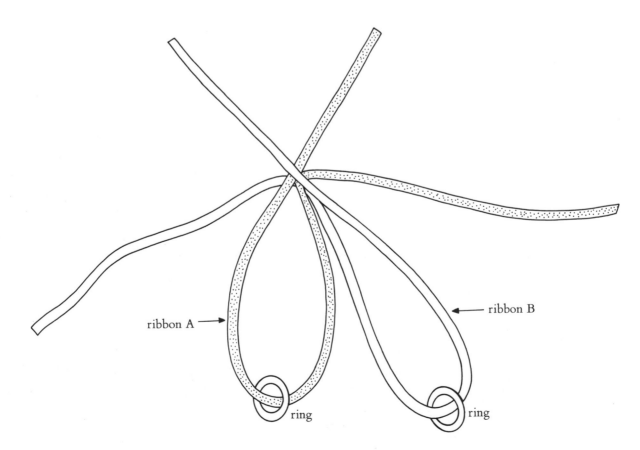

ribbon A

ribbon B

ring

ring

# CHATELAINE

MATERIALS

Cardboard

Plastic ice-cream container lid

Remnant of black velvet 30 cm x 50 cm (12″ x 20″)

Remnant of doctor's flannel or similar cream woollen fabric 5 cm x 45 cm (2″ x 18″)

Kanagawa silk thread: one card each of 91 Dark rose, 7 Medium rose, 174 Light rose, 114 Green

Size 7 straw needle

Black felt 30 cm x 30 cm (12″ x 12″)

Pelon fleece remnant

Wadding remnant

6 silver rings 4 cm (1½″) in diameter

1.4 m (1½ yd) x 4 cm (1½″) black velvet ribbon

Spray glue

Craft glue

Knitting cotton for twisted cord

INSTRUCTIONS

1. Trace templates for all embroidery pieces onto cardboard. Cut out the required number of cardboard shapes. The pieces of cardboard are used both as a template to trace from and as inserts to stiffen various parts of the project.

2. Using the cardboard templates, trace the shapes onto the wrong side of the velvet. Ensure that there is at least 3 cm (just over 1″) between each piece. (NOTE: For the needle book, there are two patterns; one for the fabric and the other for the cardboard inserts.) Draw embroidery designs on the appropriate pieces. These cardboard templates *do not* have any seam allowances.

3. Using a thread that contrasts with the velvet fabric, make a running-stitch outline of the template. This is not essential but most markers brush off during the embroidering and it is helpful to have a stitched outline just in case it is necessary to re-draw any of the design.

4. Embroider the design using a size 7 straw needle. The bullion roses have centres of three 10-twist bullions in 91. The first round is of 12-twist bullions in 7. The second-round bullions each have 14 twists and use 174. The leaves are two 9-twist bullions in 114.

5. When embroidery is complete, carefully iron it on the wrong side into a piece of self fabric. Tacking threads marking the shape of templates may now be removed.

6. Using the cardboard patterns, and centring the embroidery design, cut out velvet pieces. Remember to leave approximately a 1 cm (½″) seam allowance around each piece. Cut felt pieces the same size as the cardboard template.

7. Using spray glue, lightly spray the cardboard shapes for the needle book and scissors case and attach to pelon. For the pin cushion, also spray with glue but attach the cardboard to the thicker fleece.

8. When the fleece is dry and firmly attached to the cardboard, lightly spray the fleece and attach the shape to the appropriate embroidery piece. Remember to check that the embroidery is correctly centred. Allow to dry completely.

Patterns and Embroidery Design for Chatelaine

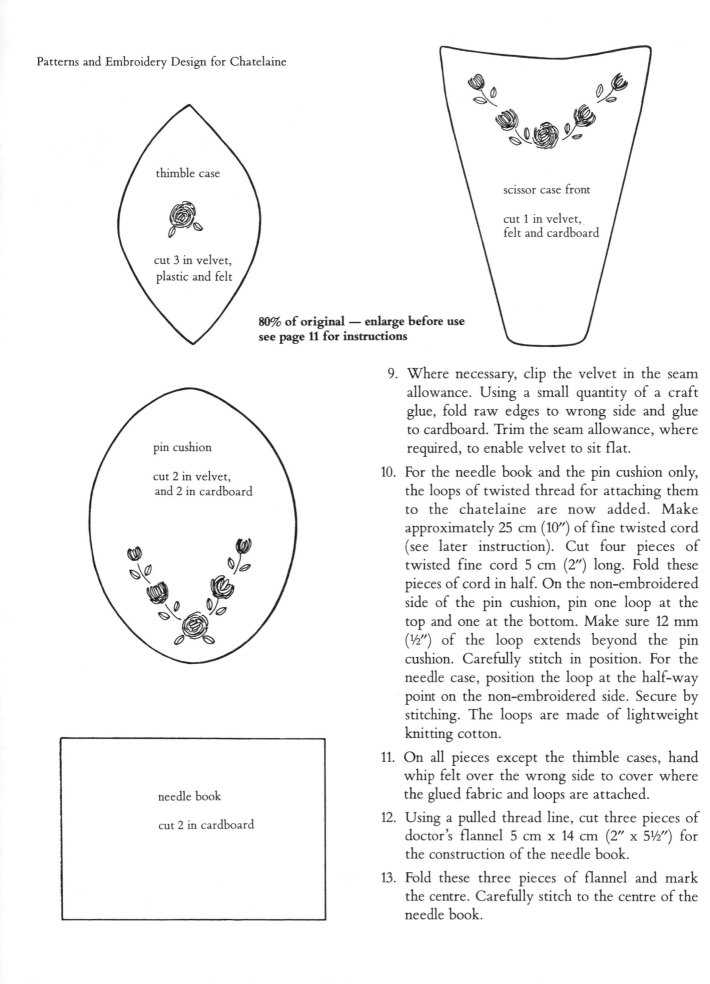

thimble case

cut 3 in velvet,
plastic and felt

**80% of original — enlarge before use
see page 11 for instructions**

scissor case front

cut 1 in velvet,
felt and cardboard

pin cushion

cut 2 in velvet,
and 2 in cardboard

needle book

cut 2 in cardboard

9. Where necessary, clip the velvet in the seam allowance. Using a small quantity of a craft glue, fold raw edges to wrong side and glue to cardboard. Trim the seam allowance, where required, to enable velvet to sit flat.

10. For the needle book and the pin cushion only, the loops of twisted thread for attaching them to the chatelaine are now added. Make approximately 25 cm (10″) of fine twisted cord (see later instruction). Cut four pieces of twisted fine cord 5 cm (2″) long. Fold these pieces of cord in half. On the non-embroidered side of the pin cushion, pin one loop at the top and one at the bottom. Make sure 12 mm (½″) of the loop extends beyond the pin cushion. Carefully stitch in position. For the needle case, position the loop at the half-way point on the non-embroidered side. Secure by stitching. The loops are made of lightweight knitting cotton.

11. On all pieces except the thimble cases, hand whip felt over the wrong side to cover where the glued fabric and loops are attached.

12. Using a pulled thread line, cut three pieces of doctor's flannel 5 cm x 14 cm (2″ x 5½″) for the construction of the needle book.

13. Fold these three pieces of flannel and mark the centre. Carefully stitch to the centre of the needle book.

Patterns and Embroidery Designs for Chatelaine

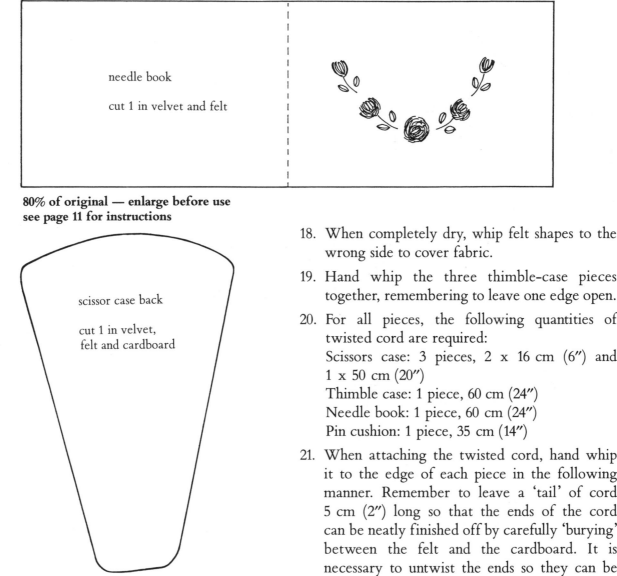

needle book

cut 1 in velvet and felt

**80% of original — enlarge before use
see page 11 for instructions**

scissor case back

cut 1 in velvet,
felt and cardboard

14. Stitch a press stud to close the needle case.

15. To make the thimble case, cut the three pattern pieces from the ice-cream container lid. It is easiest to do this by tracing around the cardboard template cut out in Step 1.

16. Spray one side of each of the plastic shapes with spray glue. Attach the appropriate embroidered pieces of velvet directly to the plastic. NOTE: There is no padding in the thimble case. Allow to dry.

17. When thoroughly dry, clip the excess fabric to permit turning in. Place sufficient craft glue on the plastic and carefully turn in the raw edge.

18. When completely dry, whip felt shapes to the wrong side to cover fabric.

19. Hand whip the three thimble-case pieces together, remembering to leave one edge open.

20. For all pieces, the following quantities of twisted cord are required:
Scissors case: 3 pieces, 2 x 16 cm (6″) and 1 x 50 cm (20″)
Thimble case: 1 piece, 60 cm (24″)
Needle book: 1 piece, 60 cm (24″)
Pin cushion: 1 piece, 35 cm (14″)

21. When attaching the twisted cord, hand whip it to the edge of each piece in the following manner. Remember to leave a 'tail' of cord 5 cm (2″) long so that the ends of the cord can be neatly finished off by carefully 'burying' between the felt and the cardboard. It is necessary to untwist the ends so they can be threaded into a needle and pushed down into the gap between the felt and cardboard. Using this method a smooth finish can be obtained.

22. For the needle case, the cord is positioned on the fold of the book because this is the most convenient location for the start and finish.

23. For the thimble case, fold the twisted cord in half. Begin at the top and use each end to stitch down one side and up the other. The two threads will then finish at the top and no joins will be necessary.

24. For the scissors case, whip the two short pieces of cord to the top back and top front; bury the ends.

25. Now whip the scissors case together.

26. Fold the long piece of cord in half and, beginning from the centre bottom, whip up both sides of the case.

27. To make up the chatelaine, take three of the six rings. The velvet ribbon is 'woven' through in the following way. Bring ribbon under the first ring and over the junction between the first and second rings as in the first diagram.

Diagram 1

28. Come up under this junction as in the second diagram. The ribbon then goes down in the space formed between the second and third rings. It is then brought up over the third ring (see diagram 2).

Diagram 2

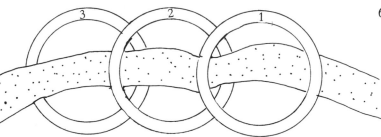

29. It may be necessary to adjust the length of ribbon to suit the wearer. Taller people usually like the ribbon longer.

30. Tie the ends of the twisted cord together on the thimble case and scissors case.

31. Fold in the raw edges of the ribbon and place the knotted end of the twisted cord on it. Fold the ribbon over and hand stitch in place.

32. Repeat for the other end of the ribbon.

33. Position needle case and pin cushion in desired location and hand stitch to the ribbon through the loops.

34. Tie other sewing accessories to rings with fine black ribbon.

MAKING A TWISTED CORD
Four-ply knitting cotton is used to make the cord for the chatelaine. The thin cord uses one piece of yarn, the thicker cords, two.

Twisted cords are easier to make with two people, so enlist the help of a friend.

1. Cut a length of cotton about seven times the required finished length of cord.

2. Knot the two ends together.

3. Insert a pencil in each of the end loops. It is important that the knot is located at one of these ends, not in the middle of the yarn.

4. Pull the thread taut and turn both the pencils clockwise until the yarn is tightly wound together. How much twist to put in is largely a matter of practice, so you may need to make a few samples first.

5. Still keeping the yarn taut, fold the twisted yarn in half and let it twist back on itself.

6. It may be necessary to run your fingers down the cord to help smooth out areas of uneven twist. When you are happy with the result, knot the previously knotted end to prevent cord from untwisting.

HOLLY BLOUSE

I love Christmas garments but always have the dilemma of what to do with them at the end of the festive season. Somehow, keeping them until next year has never appealed.

This tailored lady's blouse is as close to being the ideal solution as possible! It is made from handkerchief linen and piped in Liberty tartan. Large mother-of-pearl buttons are sewn on with bullion stitch to resemble holly.

At the end of the festive season, I simply remove the buttons (that's if I can bear to cut them off) and sew them back on using regular thread. The same idea could be used on a plain white blouse. This project is quick — a must for me at Christmas time.

MATERIALS

Either purchase a white blouse or make one from your favourite pattern. The piping trim is optional

Sufficient 18 mm (¾″) buttons (or a size to suit your buttonholes) to go down the front of the blouse. They must have four holes. It is impossible to work the holly if the buttons only have two. On the blouse I made, I omitted the button and buttonhole on the collar band. This was deliberate in order not to detract from the buttons down the front. If you are working on a purchased blouse, sew a button of the same type on the collar band with regular thread

Size 10 straw needle

Size 8 straw needle

DMC floss: 304 Red, 986 Green

These colours were chosen to match the Liberty piping but any Christmas red or green would be suitable

INSTRUCTIONS

1. Mark the position of the buttons, arranging them so that the holes are orientated as shown in the diagram.

Diagram 1

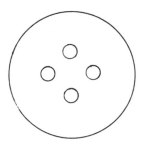

2. Using one strand of the green floss, work two 22-twist bullions in the vertical position with the size 10 straw needle.

Diagram 2

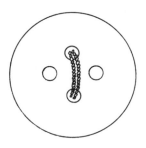

3. Now work two bullions, each with 22 twists, on one side.

Diagram 3

4. Repeat for other side.

Diagram 4

5. Go through to the back and finish off the green thread.

6. With two strands of the red thread, make about three to five French knots at the base of the six bullions with the size 8 straw needle.

Diagram 5

7. Repeat for other buttons.

CUSHIONS

RIBBON FLOWER CUSHION

MATERIALS

50 cm x 115 cm (20″ x 45″) cream grosgrain fabric

85 cm (34″) soft pink ribbon 2.5 cm (1″) wide (for two side-on flowers and five circles to make large flower)

1 m (40″) soft pink ribbon 14 mm (½″) wide

42 cm (17″) medium green ribbon 14 mm (½″) wide

60 cm (24″) dark green ribbon 14 mm (½″) wide

13 x 6 mm (¼″) pink beads for centres of flowers

10 x 3 mm (1/16″) pink beads to mix with French knots at centre of large flower

One skein of Brazilian embroidery thread, 'Iris 146' (dark pink)

One skein of Brazilian embroidery thread, 'Lola 167' (green)

Size 3 straw needle

Size 8 or 9 crewel needle for regular sewing

Thread to match ribbons and fabric

0.5 m (20″) of floral fabric to match ribbons (for frill)

1.2 m (1⅓ yd) of piping to match floral fabric

25 cm (10″) cream zipper (optional)

INSTRUCTIONS

1. Trace the design onto the wrong side of the fabric.

2. Cut the 2.5 cm (1″) soft pink ribbon into seven pieces, 10-12 cm (4″-5″) long. Cut the 14 mm (½″) soft pink ribbon into eight pieces, 10-12 cm (4″-5″) long. Cut the 14 mm (½″) medium green ribbon into seven pieces, 6 cm (2½″) long. Cut the 14 mm (½″) dark green ribbon into 10 pieces, 6 cm (2½″) long.

3. For the 2.5 cm (1″) soft pink ribbon, seam the two ends together to form a circle. Press the seam to one side.

4. In a thread to match the ribbon, run small gathering stitches by hand all the way around the circle. Make sure these stitches are close to the edge of the ribbon. Pull the gathering thread tightly to form a circle. Repeat for remaining ribbon.

5. Arrange five of these circles of ribbon as indicated by the design. Pin in position. Set the other two ribbon circles aside.

6. Repeat steps 3 and 4 for the narrower pink ribbon. Pin in position as indicated by the design.

7. To make the leaves, fold the ribbon as indicated below.

Diagram 1

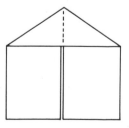

8. Run a gathering thread, in cotton to match the ribbon, as shown below.

Diagram 2

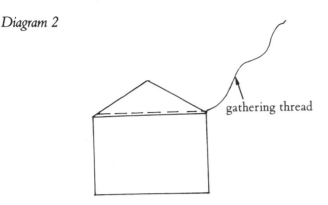

gathering thread

9. Pull up gathering thread and finish off to form a leaf.

Diagram 3

10. Repeat for all other green ribbons.

11. Distribute all but four dark green leaves, as indicated by the design.

12. To make the side-on flowers, fold one of the large ribbon circles (left over from step 5) in half across the gathered middle. Arrange the two leaves at its base to form the calyx and secure by stitching. Repeat for the other circle of ribbon. Pin to design.

13. When you are happy with the arrangement of the ribbon, carefully stitch in place. The circles that make up the large, central flower are best stitched around the outer edge of the ribbon circles. The small ribbon flowers can be stitched in the centre, and only around the outside where required.

14. Using the pink 'Iris' thread and the number 3 straw needle, make bullion roses where indicated. These roses have centres of 10 twists in the first round, 12 in the second, and 14 in the last round.

15. Work bullion leaves using the green 'Lola' thread.

16. Work sufficient French knots in the pink 'Iris' thread to cover the centre of the large flower.

17. Sew larger beads to the gathered centres of all pink ribbon. Add small beads to the French knots at the centre of the large flower.

18. Rinse the work to remove the marking pen. Allow to dry flat. Press carefully, so as not to flatten the ribbon embellishment.

19. My cushion was made up of two circles 32 cm (13″) in diameter. The embroidery was positioned 4 cm (1½″) from the bottom of the front circle. Cut front out.

20. Insert the zipper in two pieces of fabric of sufficient size to be able to cut a 32 cm (13″) circle once the zipper is in. Cut out back.

21. Pin piping around the edge of the embroidered front. Stitch in position.

22. Cut three strips of fabric 15 cm (6″) wide. Join to form a circle. Fold in half and press.

23. Run two gathering threads around the circle using a 1.5 cm (⅝″) seam allowance. Pull up.

24. Adjust gathers to fit around cushion. Baste in position.

25. With right sides together, pin front and back cushion sections together. Sew around the outside using piping stitching as a guide. Trim and neaten seam. Turn through. Press.

26. Make an insert to fit cushion.

**80% of original — enlarge before use
see page 11 for instructions**

BULLION CUSHION

This cushion was made from a remnant of fabric. The textured pattern provided an ideal frame for simple embroidery. If fabric like this is unavailable, it could be duplicated by making twin needle pintucks in a similar pattern.

The embroidered piece of fabric measures 38 cm x 27 cm (15″ x 10½″). 1.4 m (1½ yd) of braid completes the project. The embroidery is in Kanagawa 1000 silk floss. The colours are 93 Pink and 114 Green. A size 6 straw needle is used for all embroidery. All flower petals are 16 to 18-twist bullions. The buds consist of two 10-twist bullions, surrounded by two green bullions with 12 twists per stitch. The large leaves are two bullions with 12 twists per bullion. The small leaves are one 8-twist bullion. The tiny leaves at the top of the stem are two bullions with six twists in each. A small bead finishes off the centre of each flower. Small gold beads were used to highlight the diamond pattern.

INSTRUCTIONS

1. The following two designs were used to decorate this cushion.

Diagram 4

Actual size

Diagram 5

Actual size

2. These two simple motifs are arranged in the manner indicated in diagram 6.

Diagram 6

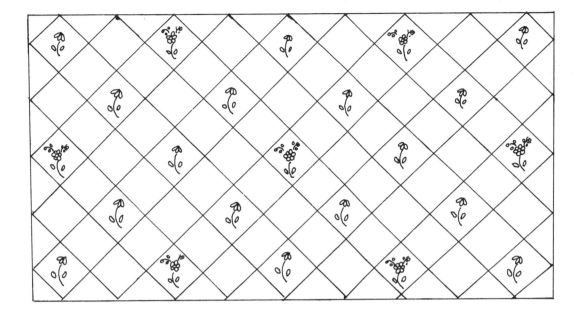

3. Complete all embroidery. Add beads to centres and diagonals, if required.

4. Rinse fabric to remove marker. Allow to dry. Press well.

5. Add a zipper to the back, if desired.

6. With the right sides together, sew back and front cushions together. Trim seam and neaten edge. Turn through to front.

7. Hand stitch braid around the cushion.

8. Make insert to fit cushion.

CRAZY PATCHWORK CUSHION

Crazy patchwork is a great way to use up scraps. Who can bear to throw out pieces of Liberty — not to mention lace? It is the ideal place to practise new stitches and try out new threads. The haphazard nature of crazy patchwork means that the embroidery stitches can be larger than normal and it does not matter if they are slightly irregular. The main thing is that the fabric and trims should be chosen for colour and texture. Let your eye be the judge!

I like to work on a piece of pre-shrunk calico (muslin) a little larger than the cushion I intend to make. Collect all your scraps. Sorting them into colours is a good idea.

How you go about laying down the fabric pieces is a matter of personal preference but I like to start in one corner and move across the project.

A quick method of seaming the patches is to press a small seam allowance on each piece and then place them on top of the calico. I then sew down each patch with clear nylon thread. To do this, thread your machine with the clear nylon thread on the top and with cream thread in the bobbin. This way, the stitching is almost invisible.

This method can be bulky if you intend using the patchwork for garments.

The better, but more time-consuming, method involves seaming each patch to the next by placing right sides together and then flipping back. This method allows seams to be trimmed so there is minimum bulk.

There are many excellent books on patchwork and you should consult one of these if you have concerns with this technique.

Almost any embroidery stitch, or combination, can be used to cover the seams in crazy patchwork.

Suggestions are feather, variations of buttonhole, lazy daisy and herringbone. Let your imagination go.

My patchwork piece measures 40 cm (16″) square when complete. The final cushion is smaller than this after seams are worked.

Finish off the cushion with pink piping (left over from Sally's Gown, see page 141) and a double frill of pink silk dupion and ecru lace (Capitol Imports lace edging 2026). These projects are great for using up that extra button or few centimetres of braid. Have fun!

ALLY'S GOWN

Embroidery need not be limited to babies' and children's garments. Treat yourself to a luxurious satin dressing gown piped in pink silk. It can make almost any morning bearable! This embroidery design is suitable for any front-wrapped robe with a shawl collar. There are many patterns available through major pattern companies. It is possible to embroider a purchased gown, but this gives less opportunity to finish the back off neatly. However it does save on construction time. The choice is yours.

MATERIALS

A suitable dressing gown in an appropriate size *or*

Sufficient cream satin fabric to make the robe and piping of your choice

2 cards Kanagawa 1000 silk thread in 93 Light pink

1 card Kanagawa 1000 silk thread in 91 Dark pink

1 card Kanagawa 1000 silk thread in 114 Green

Size 7 straw needle for bullions

Size 7 crewel needle for stem stitch

Fabric marker of your choice

INSTRUCTIONS

1. Remove the shawl-collar piece from your pattern.

2. Position the embroidery design on the collar section so that it can be satisfactorily cut out. In general, the embroidery design needs to be located about 5 cm (2") below the shoulder and above where the collars will cross each other. It is a good idea to trace the pattern onto some lightweight interfacing and then to trace the embroidery design onto this pattern. This way, it is possible to check your positioning. Sometimes it will be necessary to leave out certain parts of the design so it will fit on your pattern. Remember that the embroidery design will need to be reversed for the other lapel. The simplest method for doing this is to trace the design onto some tracing paper and then place the tracing paper with its right side down. A perfectly reversed design may now be traced onto the garment.

3. Once you have decided on the positioning of the embroidery design, trace it onto the fabric in the desired location. Repeat for the other lapel. As satin frays easily, it is a good idea to finish the edges of the fabric by either zigzagging or serging (using an overlocker).

4. The size 7 straw needle is used for all bullions and the crewel needle for all stem stitching. The Kanagawa 1000 silk thread is used as it comes off the card in a single strand.

5. The daisy petals are in 93 Light pink and have 10 wraps per bullion. The centres are French knots in 91 Dark pink.

6. The flame flower has its base five petals in 91. The four side petals have 10 twists per bullion. The central base petal is made up of a 12-twist bullion. The two extending petals are in 93 and have approximately 14 wraps in the shorter petal and 16 in the longer. The green base is a 12-twist bullion in 114.

Sally's Gown — Top Half of Embroidery Design

join to bottom half of embroidery design on this line – **Actual size**

Sally's Gown — Bottom Half of Embroidery Design

join to top half of embroidery design on this line _ _ _ _ _ _ _ _ _ _ _ _ _ _ _ _

Actual size

7. There are many leaves in this design. The larger leaves are comprised of two bullion stitches with 12 twists per bullion in 114.

8. The smaller leaves are single bullions with nine twists. There are two bullions with seven wraps each at the tops of stems.

9. Complete all embroidery. Rinse the fabric to remove the markings. Allow to dry flat. Iron with a warm iron and pressing cloth, on the wrong side. Make sure that the right side is supported by a thick, soft towel to protect the embroidery.

10. Cut out pattern piece and remainder of garment. Make up as per pattern instructions.